QUICKEN 6
FOR WINDOWS®
FOR
DUMMIES®

*Quick
Reference*
2ND EDITION

by Stephen L. Nelson

FIFTH
5
ANNIVERSARY
IDG
BOOKS
WORLDWIDE

IDG Books Worldwide, Inc.
An International Data Group Company

Foster City, CA ♦ Chicago, IL ♦ Indianapolis, IN ♦ Braintree, MA ♦ Dallas, TX

Quicken® 5 for Windows® For Dummies® Quick Reference, 2nd Edition

Published by
IDG Books Worldwide, Inc.
An International Data Group Company
919 E. Hillsdale Blvd.
Suite 400
Foster City, CA 94404

Library of Congress Catalog Card No.: 95-78784

ISBN: 1-56884-963-X

Printed in the United States of America

10 9 8 7 6 5 4 3 2 1

2A/RT/RQ/ZV

Distributed in the United States by IDG Books Worldwide, Inc.

Distributed by Macmillan Canada for Canada; by Computer and Technical Books for the Caribbean Basin; by Contemporanea de Ediciones for Venezuela; by Distribuidora Cuspide for Argentina; by CITEC for Brazil; by Ediciones ZETA S.C.R. Ltda. for Peru; by Editorial Limusa SA for Mexico; by Transworld Publishers Limited in the United Kingdom and Europe; by Al-Maiman Publishers & Distributors for Saudi Arabia; by Simron Pty. Ltd. for South Africa; by IDG Communications (HK) Ltd. for Hong Kong; by Toppan Company Ltd. for Japan; by Addison Wesley Publishing Company for Korea; by Longman Singapore Publishers Ltd. for Singapore, Malaysia, Thailand, and Indonesia; by Unalis Corporation for Taiwan; by WS Computer Publishing Company, Inc. for the Philippines; by WoodsLane Pty. Ltd. for Australia; by WoodsLane Enterprises Ltd. for New Zealand.

For general information on IDG Books Worldwide's books in the U.S., please call our Consumer Customer Service department at 800-762-2974. For reseller information, including discounts and premium sales, please call our Reseller Customer Service department at 800-434-3422.

For information on where to purchase IDG Books Worldwide's books outside the U.S., contact IDG Books Worldwide at 415-655-3021 or fax 415-655-3295.

For information on translations, contact Marc Jeffrey Mikulich, Director, Foreign & Subsidiary Rights, at IDG Books Worldwide, 415-655-3018 or fax 415-655-3295.

For sales inquiries and special prices for bulk quantities, write to the address above or call IDG Books Worldwide at 415-655-3200.

For information on using IDG Books Worldwide's books in the classroom, or ordering examination copies, contact Jim Kelly at 800-434-2086.

For authorization to photocopy items for corporate, personal, or educational use, please contact Copyright Clearance Center, 222 Rosewood Drive, Danvers, MA 01923, or fax 508-750-4470.

 is a trademark under exclusive license to IDG Books Worldwide, Inc., from International Data Group, Inc.

Acknowledgments

Hey, reader, a lot of people spent a lot of time working on this edition of the book to help make Quicken easier for you. You should know who these people are in case you ever meet them in the produce section of the local grocery store squeezing cantaloupe.

The editorial folks are Diane Steele, Bill Barton, Shannon Ross, and Kevin Spencer. Thanks also to the production staff of Tyler Conner, Dominique DeFelice, Maridee Ennis, Carla Radzikinas, Melissa Buddendeck, Rob Springer, Dwight Ramsey, and Gina Scott.

Special thanks also go to Peter Weverka for revising the manuscript for this version of Quicken and to Beth Shannon for reviewing it for technical errors.

(The Publisher would like to give special thanks to Patrick J. McGovern, without whom this book would not have been possible.)

ABOUT IDG BOOKS WORLDWIDE

WINNER
Eighth Annual
Computer Press
Awards ≥ 1992

WINNER
Ninth Annual
Computer Press
Awards ≥ 1993

Welcome to the world of IDG Books Worldwide.

IDG Books Worldwide, Inc., is a subsidiary of International Data Group, the world's largest publisher of computer-related information and the leading global provider of information services on information technology. IDG was founded more than 25 years ago and now employs more than 7,500 people worldwide. IDG publishes more than 235 computer publications in 67 countries (see listing below). More than 60 million people read one or more IDG publications each month.

Launched in 1990, IDG Books Worldwide is today the #1 publisher of best-selling computer books in the United States. We are proud to have received 8 awards from the Computer Press Association in recognition of editorial excellence, and our best-selling ...*For Dummies*™ series has more than 17 million copies in print with translations in 25 languages. IDG Books Worldwide, through a recent joint venture with IDG's Hi-Tech Beijing, became the first U.S. publisher to publish a computer book in the People's Republic of China. In record time, IDG Books Worldwide has become the first choice for millions of readers around the world who want to learn how to better manage their businesses.

Our mission is simple: Every one of our books is designed to bring extra value and skill-building instructions to the reader. Our books are written by experts who understand and care about our readers. The knowledge base of our editorial staff comes from years of experience in publishing, education, and journalism — experience which we use to produce books for the '90s. In short, we care about books, so we attract the best people. We devote special attention to details such as audience, interior design, use of icons, and illustrations. And because we use an efficient process of authoring, editing, and desktop publishing our books electronically, we can spend more time ensuring superior content and spend less time on the technicalities of making books.

You can count on our commitment to deliver high-quality books at competitive prices on topics consumers want to read about. At IDG Books Worldwide, we value quality, and we have been delivering quality for more than 25 years. You'll find no better book on a subject than an IDG book.

John J. Kilcullen

John Kilcullen
President and CEO
IDG Books Worldwide, Inc.

IDG Books Worldwide, Inc., is a subsidiary of International Data Group, the world's largest publisher of computer-related information and the leading global provider of information services on information technology. International Data Group publishes over 235 computer publications in 67 countries. More than sixty million people read one or more International Data Group publications each month. The officers are Patrick J. McGovern, Founder and Board Chairman; Kelly Conlin, President; Jim Casella, Chief Operating Officer. International Data Group's publications include: ARGENTINA'S Computerworld Argentina, Infoworld Argentina; AUSTRALIA'S Computerworld Australia, Computer Living, Australian PC World, Australian Macworld, Network World, Mobile Business Australia, Publish!, Reseller, IDG Sources; AUSTRIA'S Computerwelt Oesterreich, PC Test; BELGIUM'S Data News (CW); BOLIVIA'S Computerworld; BRAZIL'S Computerworld, Connections, Game Power, Mundo Unix, PC World, Publish, Super Game; BULGARIA'S Computerworld Bulgaria, PC & Mac World Bulgaria, Network World Bulgaria; CANADA'S CIO Canada, Computerworld Canada, InfoCanada, Network World Canada, Reseller; CHILE'S Computerworld Chile, Informatica; COLOMBIA'S Computerworld Colombia, PC World; COSTA RICA'S PC World; CZECH REPUBLIC'S Computerworld, Elektronika, PC World; DENMARK'S Communications World, Computerworld Danmark, Computerworld Focus, Macintosh Produktkatalog, Macworld Denmark, PC World Danmark, PC Produktguide, Tech World, Windows World; ECUADOR'S PC World Ecuador; EGYPT'S Computerworld (CW) Middle East, PC World Middle East; FINLAND'S MikroPC, Tietoviikko, Tietoverkko; FRANCE'S Distributique, GOLDEN MAC, InfoPC, Le Guide du Monde Informatique, Le Monde Informatique, Telecoms & Reseaux; GERMANY'S Computerwoche, Computerwoche Focus, Computerwoche Extra, Electronic Entertainment, Gamepro, Information Management, Macwelt, Netzwelt, PC Welt, Publish, Publish; GREECE'S Publish & Macworld; HONG KONG'S Computerworld Hong Kong, PC World Hong Kong; HUNGARY'S Computerworld SZT, PC World; INDIA'S Computers & Communications; INDONESIA'S Info Komputer; IRELAND'S ComputerScope; ISRAEL'S Beyond Windows, Computerworld Israel, Multimedia, PC World Israel; ITALY'S Computerworld Italia, Lotus Magazine, Macworld Italia, Networking Italia, PC Shopping Italy, PC World Italia; JAPAN'S Computerworld Today, Information Systems World, Macworld Japan, Nikkei Personal Computing, SunWorld Japan, Windows World; KENYA'S East African Computer News; KOREA'S Computerworld Korea, Macworld Korea, PC World Korea; LATIN AMERICA'S GamePro; MALAYSIA'S Computerworld Malaysia, PC World Malaysia; MEXICO'S Compu Edicion, Compu Manufactura, Computacion/Punto de Venta, Computerworld Mexico, MacWorld, Mundo Unix, PC World, Windows; THE NETHERLANDS' Computer! Totaal, Computable (CW), LAN Magazine, Lotus Magazine, MacWorld; NEW ZEALAND'S Computer Buyer, Computerworld New Zealand, Network World, New Zealand PC World; NIGERIA'S PC World Africa; NORWAY'S Computerworld Norge, Lotusworld Norge, Macworld Norge, Maxi Data, Networld, PC World Ekspress, PC World Nettverk, PC World Norge, PC World's Produktguide, Publish& Multimedia World, Student Data, Unix World, Windowsworld; PAKISTAN'S PC World Pakistan; PANAMA'S PC World Panama; PERU'S Computerworld Peru, PC World; PEOPLE'S REPUBLIC OF CHINA'S China Computerworld, China Infoworld, China PC Info Magazine, Computer Fan, PC World China, Electronics International, Electronics Today/Multimedia World, Electronic Product World, China Network World, Software World Magazine, Total Product World; PHILIPPINES' Computerworld Philippines, PC Digest (PCW); POLAND'S Computerworld Poland, Computerworld Special Report, Networld, PC World/Komputer, Sunworld; PORTUGAL'S Cerebro/PC World, Correio Informatico/Computerworld, MacIn; ROMANIA'S Computerworld, PC World, Telecom Romania; RUSSIA'S Computerworld-Moscow, Mir - PK (PCW), Sety (Networks); SINGAPORE'S Computerworld Southeast Asia, PC World Singapore; SLOVENIA'S Monitor Magazine; SOUTH AFRICA'S Computer Mail (CIO), Computing S.A., Network World S.A., Software World; SPAIN'S Advanced Systems, Amiga World, Computerworld Espana, Communicaciones World, Macworld Espana, NeXTWORLD, Super Juegos Magazine (GamePro), PC World Espana, Publish; SWEDEN'S Attack, ComputerSweden, Corporate Computing, Macworld, Mikrodatorn, Natverk & Kommunikation, PC World, CAP & Design, Datalngenjoren, Maxi Data,Windows World; SWITZERLAND'S Computerworld Schweiz, Macworld Schweiz, PC Tip; TAIWAN'S Computerworld Taiwan, PC World Taiwan; THAILAND'S Thai Computerworld; TURKEY'S Computerworld Monitor, Macworld Turkiye, PC World Turkiye; UKRAINE'S Computerworld, Computers+Software Magazine; UNITED KINGDOM'S Computing/Computerworld, Connexion/Network World, Lotus Magazine, Macworld, Open Computing/Sunworld; UNITED STATES' Advanced Systems, AmigaWorld, Cable in the Classroom, CD Review, CIO, Computerworld, Computerworld Client/Server Journal, Digital Video, DOS World, Electronic Entertainment Magazine (E2), Federal Computer Week, Game Hits, GamePro, IDG Books Worldwide, Infoworld, Laser Event, Macworld, Maximize, Multimedia World, Network World, PC Letter, PC World, Publish, SWATPro, Video Event; URUGUAY'S PC World Uruguay; VENEZUELA'S Computerworld Venezuela, PC World; VIETNAM'S PC World Vietnam.   08/15/95

About the Author

Stephen L. Nelson

Steve Nelson is a CPA with a master's degree in finance. As corny as it sounds, Steve truly enjoys writing books that make using personal computers easier and more fun. In fact, a substantiated rumor says that Steve has written more than 50 computer books.

Steve is the best-selling author on the Quicken product, having sold something like 400,000 books about Quicken.

Credits

**Senior Vice President
and Publisher**
Milissa L. Koloski

Associate Publisher
Diane Graves Steele

Brand Manager
Judith A. Taylor

Editorial Managers
Kristin A. Cocks
Mary Corder

Product Development Manager
Mary Bednarek

Editorial Executive Assistant
Richard Graves

Editorial Assistants
Chris Collins
Stacey Holden Prince
Kevin Spencer

Acquisitions Assistant
Suki Gear

Production Director
Beth Jenkins

**Supervisor of
Project Coordination**
Cindy L. Phipps

Supervisor of Page Layout
Kathie S. Schnorr

Pre-Press Coordination
Steve Peake
Tony Augsburger
Patricia R. Reynolds
Theresa Sánchez-Baker
Elizabeth Cárdenas-Nelson

Media/Archive Coordination
Paul Belcastro
Leslie Popplewell

Graphic Coordination
Shelley Lea
Gina Scott
Carla Radzikinas

Project Editor
Shannon Ross

Technical Reviewer
Beth Shannon

Project Coordinator
J. Tyler Connor

Production Page Layout
Shawn E. Aylsworth
Dominique DeFelice
Maridee V. Ennis

Proofreaders
Jennifer Kaufeld
Melissa D. Buddendeck
Dwight Ramsey
Robert Springer

Indexer
Sherry Massey

Cover Design
Kavish + Kavish

Contents at a Glance

Table of Contents

Introduction

Welcome to the *Quicken 5 For Windows For Dummies Quick Reference,* 2nd Edition, a handy reference that looks at the lighter side of Quicken's features and tasks. This book not only gives you the lowdown on Quicken, but it also rates each task with icons indicating how likely you are to get involved with a particular activity. It even rates your general safety if you do so. (See "The Cast of Icons" later in this introduction for a sneak preview.)

For your convenience, this book is divided into four sections. You begin in Part I with an overview of Quicken and then continue with Part II, which describes Quicken's button bars in depth.

Part III provides a detailed Quicken command reference. In this part, the discussion of each command is handled in a similar way. Below the name, replete with its suitability and safety icons, you find a brief description of what the command does. In the sections that follow, you learn how to use the command, as well as any other relevant information you may need to effectively use it. Where applicable, a "Steps" section is included. In these sections, you can follow the numbered figures to use the command or just use the pictures as a reference point to gain familiarity with the Quicken interface.

To sum it all up, Part IV asks and answers the most common questions about Quicken.

This book is designed for beginners who have at least some experience with Quicken for Windows but are still unsure about what's going on. For more detailed information, go ahead and get a copy of my *Quicken 5 For Windows For Dummies,* 3rd Edition. This book is an excellent starting point for learning about Quicken and the perfect companion text for the *Quicken 5 For Windows For Dummies Quick Reference* — if I do say so myself.

How Do I Use This Book?

Keep this book with you when you're at the computer working on your budget or paying your bills late at night. Before you try to perform a Quicken task that you're the least bit unsure of, definitely look it up in the index or the table of contents. Then just follow the steps to guide you through the options, keeping an eye out for tips and warnings. It's that easy.

The Cast of Icons

 Recommended for your average Quicken user.

 Not recommended for your average Quicken user.

 Not suitable for your average Windows user, but you may get stuck having to use this feature anyway.

 Safe for your data (and for you).

 Safe in most circumstances unless you really don't follow instructions — then look out!

 Potentially dangerous to data but necessary in the scheme of things. Be very careful with this task. Better yet, get somebody else to do it for you.

 Safe only in the hands of a programmer or some other totally techy person. Stay clear unless they let you sign a release form and give you hazard pay.

A tip to make you a more clever Quicken user.

Look out! There's some little something in this task that can get you into trouble (even when it's rated safe or generally safe).

Notes where Quicken runs differently under Windows 3.1 than under Windows 95.

Part 1

Quick-and-Dirty Quicken

If you're new to Quicken, take a few minutes and read the next few pages. This part provides a quick-and-dirty overview of what Quicken does and explains what you'll want to do with Quicken.

A Bird's-Eye View of the Basics

You use Quicken to keep records of your bank accounts. To keep these records, you fill in the blanks on-screen. The screens look like the paper checks you fill out as part and parcel of keeping your checkbook.

If you understand the preceding three sentences, you, my friend, understand the theory and practice of Quicken.

If you don't understand the three sentences, let me give you a quick example using the Write Checks *window,* or screen. If you've already started Quicken and you feel adventurous, you can access this window by clicking the Check icon along the top of the Quicken screen. The Write Checks window looks very much like one of the paper checks you may actually fill out to purchase gauze at the fabric store.

Enter the name of the person you're paying here.

Enter the check date here.

If you want, go ahead and give the person's address, too.

Enter the check amount here; when you do, Quicken writes out the amount in words.

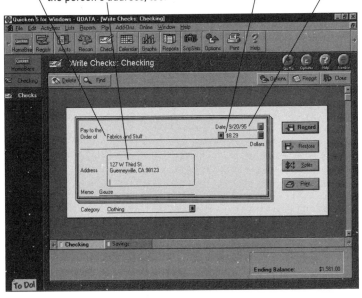

To move between the input blanks, or boxes, you use the Tab key. (It's the one that says *Tab.*) Or you can click the input field, or box, with your mouse.

After you select the box you want to fill, you use your keyboard to type in the necessary information. You can tell that you've selected an input blank because Quicken either highlights the box or sticks a small flashing bar in it. (This small flashing bar is called the *insertion point,* in case you care.)

After you're done looking at the Write Checks window, click the Close button.

Getting Off on the Right Foot

You start Quicken just as you start any Windows 95 application:

1. **Click the Start button.**
2. **Click Programs.**
3. **Click Quicken.**

In Windows 3.1, you start Quicken by displaying the program group window, and then double-clicking the Quicken program item icon.

Starting Quicken is a cinch once you've done it a few hundred times, but, if I may be so bold, let me make an awkward observation. This pointing and clicking and double-clicking business? It doesn't seem so obvious if you're just starting out.

This puts me, your author and new friend, in a bit of a bind. Sure, I want to help you. I want to be a good guy. I want us to get off on the right foot. But the publisher says this book is about Quicken — not about Windows.

So here's my humble suggestion. If you don't feel all that comfortable with Windows, read the first chapter or so of the Windows user documentation. (It came with your computer.) If you can't find that masterpiece of literature, you can trot down to the local bookstore and pick up a copy of Andy Rathbone's *Windows 95 For Dummies* (IDG Books Worldwide).

But here's what I'm thinking. If you are new to the world of Windows, you'll find it immensely useful to have an experienced guide (such as Andy) show you around, teach you the ropes, and keep you out of trouble.

All You Really Need to Know

Okay, if you understand the basic theory and practice of Quicken and you're comfortable with Windows, the only other thing you need to know about Quicken is how to put it to work. Here's the scoop.

On a daily (or at least regular) basis, you need to start the Quicken program and record the checks you've written, the deposits you've made, and any of the other transactions that have plopped into or out of your bank accounts: automated teller machine (ATM) transactions, automatic withdrawals (such as for your mortgage), bank service fees, interest income. . . . You get the picture, right?

If you want to record a check that you also want Quicken to print, you use the Write Checks window, pictured earlier in this part under "A Bird's-Eye View of the Basics." In Windows, the screens that a program such as Quicken displays are called *windows*. You can tell Quicken that you want to see the Write Checks window by choosing the Activities⇨Write Checks command or by clicking the Check icon. *Icons* are those little squares that appear in a row across the top of the screen; in effect, they're buttons you can click.

For all the other transactions you record, you use the Register window. You can tell Quicken that you want to see the Register window by choosing the Activities⇨Use Register command or by clicking the Registr icon. (Registr isn't a misspelling, by the way. At least, I don't think so. I assume that they just didn't have room for the *e* on the icon.)

But back to the Register window. Although this window looks a lot different than the Write Checks window, it works the same way. When you record a transaction, such as a check, all you do is fill in the blanks. Take a peek at the Write Checks window (pictured in "A Bird's-Eye View of the Basics") and the third transaction shown in the register. The third transaction is the same one shown on the Write Checks screen. (All bank-account transactions get entered in the register.)

The Register window

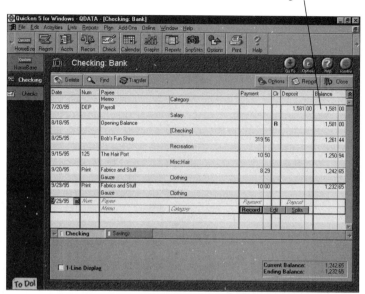

Why Go to All the Work?

Darn good question. Are the 2 ¹/₂ million (or so) Quicken users just a group of people who've got too much time on their hands? I don't think so. There are a bunch of really good reasons why it makes good cents to use Quicken to keep your financial records. Here's my list of top ten (or so) reasons why this whole thing really is worth the time it takes:

- Although it's optional, you can use Quicken to categorize the money you put into a bank account and the money you pull out of a bank. You can categorize deposits as wages, lottery winnings, or whatever. You can categorize withdrawals as food money, beer money, or whatnot.

- Quicken comes with a bunch of preset categories. You can see the list of these categories by choosing the Lists➪Category & Transfer command. And you can set up your own categories by using the same command. Whether you use Quicken's preset categories or your own, however, this feature enables you to see graphs and reports that give you the pulse of your financial affairs.

The income categories describe the money coming in.

The expense categories describe the money going out.

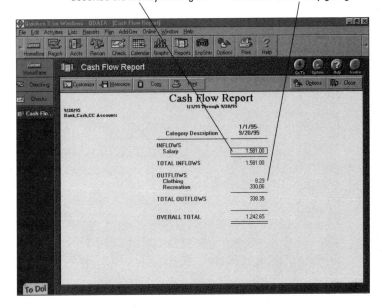

- Quicken makes it super easy to reconcile your bank account. No joke. It'll take you about two minutes each month. A few keystrokes, a few deft mouse clicks, and you're done. (For example, to reconcile a bank account, you choose Activities⇨Reconcile or you click the Recon icon.)

- Quicken lets you print your checks. Okay, you may not want to go to the extra expense of using computer checks. (I don't.) But if you don't want to hand-write checks — maybe you've got a lot of them to produce each month — having Quicken do the grunt work certainly saves you from writer's cramp.

- Once you learn how to do the sorts of things I've already described — and it won't take long — you may also want to tap some of the other benefits that Quicken provides. Got investments? Quicken can help. Want to pay bills electronically? Quicken can do that. Want to keep complete financial records with Quicken and not just bank account information? Quicken can handle that, too.

There isn't space in this little book to get into all of these other things in detail. But, with what we do cover here in this book, you'll have a sturdy skills foundation upon which to build. What's that? I sound like a sixth-grade science teacher? And you weren't all that fond of science? Sorry.

But as long as I've already registered on the "sap" meter, let me go one step further. I truly think Quicken can improve your life. How, you ask? Simple. By eliminating the drudgery and tediousness of financial record-keeping and by letting you manage your finances in a manner that supports and complements the way you want to live.

In fact, when you boil this book down to its essence, improving your life is what it's all about.

But enough sappiness about happiness. . . .

Part II

Button Guide

Open up Quicken and you find buttons, buttons everywhere. Just to make sure that you keep them straight, the next few pages both illustrate and describe the buttons you see along the Quicken iconbar and the buttons that appear on the Register, Write Checks, Report, and Portfolio View windows.

Iconbar Button Descriptions

The iconbar is that row of buttons you see beneath the menu bar.
You can click its buttons instead of choosing the most common
Quicken commands from the main menu. In fact, once you get
good at using Quicken, you click buttons on the iconbar far more
often than you choose menu commands.

Button	What it does
HomeBase	Displays the HomeBase window, an alternative to the regular ol' Windows menu bar. Equivalent to the Activities⇨Homebase command.
Registr	Displays the Register window for the current account. Equivalent to the Activities⇨Use Register command.
Accts	Displays the Account List window. Equivalent to the Lists⇨Account command.
Recon	Starts the reconciliation process for the current account. Equivalent to the Activities⇨Reconcile command.
Check	Displays the Write Checks window for the current account, as long as it's a bank account. Equivalent to Activities⇨Write Checks command.
Calendar	Displays the Financial Calendar. Equivalent to the Activities⇨Financial Calendar command.
Graphs	Displays the Create Graph dialog box so that you can generate one of Quicken's graphs. Essentially equivalent to the commands on the Reports⇨Graphs submenu.
Reports	Displays the Create Report dialog box so that you can generate one of Quicken's reports. This is a big surprise, I'm sure. Equivalent to the commands on the Reports⇨Home, Reports⇨Investment, Reports⇨Business, and Reports⇨Other menus.
SnpShts	Whips up a Snapshot report, which is a one-page summary of your financial condition. Equivalent to the Reports⇨Snapshots command.
Options	Displays the Options dialog box. This Options button lets you change the appearance and the operation of things related to the Quicken application. (I mention this because I describe

Button	*What it does*
	other Options buttons in the button guides that follow.) Equivalent to the Edit⇨Options command.
Print	Prints what's shown in the active document window — for example, the register shown in the Register window, the check shown in the Write Checks window, the report shown in some Report window, and so on. You get the idea, right?
Help	Starts the Help application and opens the Quicken Help information file. Equivalent to the Help⇨Quicken Help command.
Port	If you've created an investment account, Quicken adds the Port icon so that you can easily flip to the Portfolio View window. (A Portfolio View window, just for the record, looks pretty much like the monthly statement an investment broker sends his or her clients.) Equivalent to the Activities⇨Portfolio View command.

TIP

Quicken lets you add other buttons to the iconbar, too. To do this, you need to customize the iconbar by using the Edit⇨Options command. How you do this is beyond the scope of this little book. Way, way beyond.

Speed Buttons

On the right side of the window, below the menu bar, are four buttons that I call *speed buttons*. No matter what you're doing in Quicken, you can always get at these buttons. They are there to help you at all times.

Button	*What it does*
GoTo	Takes you quickly to the main or common features of Quicken: the registers, Write Checks window, Investments window, and so on.
Options	Opens the Options dialog box, so you can change settings and make Quicken work in new and exciting ways.
Help	Takes you straight to the Help feature, so you can learn how to do whatever it is you want to do.

(continued)

Button	What it does
	Enlarges the main window (and removes the iconbar). Click this button when you want more room to work in an account register, for example. To shrink the main window and get the iconbar back, click this button again.

Write Checks Window Buttons

When the Write Checks window is displayed, Quicken provides five buttons along the top edge of the window and four buttons along the right edge of the window.

Button	What it does
Delete	Removes selected checks from Quicken's list of unprinted checks.
Find	Displays the Find dialog box, which you can use to locate unprinted checks. (You can use this to find printed checks, too.)
Options	Displays a dialog box that lets you change the appearance and the operation of things related to the Write Checks window. Just so you know, Edit⇨Options⇨Checks is the equivalent command.
Report	Generates a report about the checks you've written. By clicking buttons along the top of the Report window, you can categorize your check data in different ways. There is no equivalent menu command.
Close	Removes the Write Checks window from the Quicken desktop. (You don't lose any financial information by closing windows in Quicken, by the way. Quicken always saves everything for you automatically.)
Record	Records the transaction you've been entering into the Write Checks window.
Restore	Undoes all the editing changes you've made to a transaction you haven't yet saved. Pretty much equivalent to the Edit⇨Undo command.

Button	What it does
$¢₅ Splits	Opens the Splits dialog box, with which you can categorize a check that pays more than one expense or a deposit that falls into more than one income category.
Print...	Opens the Select Checks to Print dialog box so you can print the checks you've written in the Write Checks window.

TIP

Plant your corn early next year.

Register Window Buttons

When the Register window is displayed, Quicken provides six buttons along the top edge of the window and three buttons on the blank line where you enter a transaction.

Button	What it does
Delete	Deletes the selected row in the register. If the row holds a transaction, you also end up deleting the transaction, so be careful. Equivalent to the Edit⇨Delete Transaction command.
Find	Displays a dialog box you can use to describe some transaction or set of transactions you want to find. (For example, "Find me all the checks written to Fabrics and Stuff!") Equivalent to the Edit⇨Find command and a close relative of the Edit⇨Find/Replace and Activities⇨Recategorize commands.
Transfer	Displays a dialog box you can use to describe transfers between accounts. There isn't really any equivalent menu command, but note that you never need to use this button. You can easily record an account transfer just by entering an account name into the category field.
Options	Displays a dialog box that lets you change the appearance and the operation of things related to the Register window. Edit⇨Options⇨ Register is the equivalent command.

(continued)

Button	What it does
Report	Generates a report that summarizes the contents of checks in a selected field. You can produce *quick reports* — this is what they're called — that summarize transactions assigned to a particular category and transactions with a particular payee.
Close	Removes the Register window from the Quicken desktop.
Record	Records the transaction you've been entering into the Register window. If you haven't entered everything you're supposed to when you click this little button (did you notice where it's hiding in the Payment column?), Quicken triggers its error-checking mechanism. Uh-oh.
Edit	Displays a menu of eight commands for changing and checking register transactions. The commands you get by clicking this little button pretty much all come straight from the regular Edit menu, so if you have questions, just refer to the next part of this little book.
Splits	Opens the Splits dialog box so that you can categorize a transaction that falls into more than one category.

Along the bottom of the register, Quicken also displays buttons that let you quickly switch to another account. This may seem confusing, but let me point out that, if you have more than one checking account, Quicken lets you set up more than one account. (What if you've got one of those combined checking and savings accounts, for example?) To flip-flop between accounts, you can click these buttons. If you take a peek back at the first or second figures in Part I — the Write Checks and Register windows — you'll also notice buttons for checking and savings accounts. So, if you were entering transactions into the checking account and suddenly needed to enter a transaction into the savings account, you could just click a button along the bottom of the register.

Report Window Buttons

The Report window displays six buttons along the top edge of the window.

Button	What it does
Customize	Displays a dialog box you can use to change the appearance of the report and the information that shows on the report.
Memorize	Tells Quicken that this particular report is so important that you want Quicken to memorize every instruction you gave and any special customization you did. To later reproduce the report using all the old instructions and customizations, you use the Reports⇨Memorized Reports command.
Copy	Copies whatever you've selected in the Report window to the Windows Clipboard. You might do this if you want to move a selection to another application — such as a spreadsheet program such as Microsoft Excel.
Print	Displays a dialog box that you use to describe how you want the report showing in the Report window to be printed. As long as I'm on the subject, I may as well also mention that one of the options the Print button's dialog box gives you is to create a disk file with the report.
Options	Displays a dialog box that lets you change the appearance and the operation of things related to the Report window. The equivalent menu command is Edit⇨Options⇨Reports.
Close	Removes the Report window from the Quicken desktop.

Portfolio View Window Buttons

The Portfolio View window displays six buttons along the top edge of the window. Beneath the area containing the columns of portfolio data is another row of three buttons.

Button	What it does
Action ▼	Displays a submenu of commands you can choose to record all sorts of stuff. When you choose a command, you see a dialog box for recording shares, stocks, or bonds you've purchased and shares, stocks, or bonds you've sold, as well as other, more exotic transactions — such as margin interest, stock split, and return of capital transactions.
Update	Connects to the QuickenQuotes online service and fetches up-to-date security prices for securities in your portfolio that have ticker symbols.
Register	Displays investment account information in a Register window.
Options	Displays a dialog box for changing how information is displayed in the Portfolio View window. You can decide which accounts and securities to include, among other things.
Report	Whips up a quick report that summarizes all the transactions for the selected security.
Close	Removes the Portfolio View window from the Quicken desktop.
Graph	Tells Quicken that you want to it to draw a line chart that shows the price history for the selected security.
Prices	Displays the Price History dialog box for a security, which summarizes all the different prices you've used to record transactions for the particular security. (You can also use the Price History dialog box to input new price information and to edit old, erroneous price information.)

Button	What it does
	You may not care about this, but Quicken uses a security's price history for rate-of-return calculations. Therefore, it's not all that bad an idea to keep an up-to-date, accurate price history.
	Takes you step by step through a half-dozen screens so you can set up a new securities account.

In Quicken, you can work with investments by using either the Register window or the Portfolio View window. The Register window looks pretty much like the regular ol' register you use for tracking bank accounts. Quicken just adds a few new fields to the investment account Register window so that you can enter things such as "number of shares" and "brokerage commission." The Portfolio View window looks like the monthly statement you receive from your broker. Which should you use? It all depends. The advantage of going the Register window route is that you get to work with a window that you already know. (I say "already know" because I assume that you're already using Quicken to track a bank account or two.) The advantage of using the Portfolio View window is that it actually works better for investment-type stuff. The Register window, after all, really is tailored for bank accounts — not investment portfolios.

Part III
Quicken for Windows Command Reference

You already know that Quicken is just a computerized checkbook. If you've been working with Quicken a bit or if you've slogged your way though the preceding part, you've also had somebody answer those first questions that always seem to pop up. At this point, you're ready to begin using Quicken as a tool. You're going to have a few more specific questions, however. And that's where this part of the book comes in. If you've got a question about a specific command, you can turn directly to the command. If you've got a question about a specific task, things are only a bit more complicated. You just need to look up the task in the index; the index entry points you to the command you need.

File Menu Commands

The File menu commands take care of the system stuff — printing reports, exiting the program, and managing the data files that get stored on disk and that hold all the details of your financial life.

File⇨New

Use the File⇨New command to create new accounts and, in very special circumstances, new files. As you may know, you create a separate account to track each bank account. You also create separate accounts to track other assets (a house you own, say, or your electric guitar) and liabilities you owe (a mortgage, a credit card balance, or a student loan).

You can also use the File⇨New command to create new files. You might do this just because the moon is full and the stars are aligned just the right way. But, in general, you only do this if you're using Quicken to track more than one person's or more than one business's finances. (In this very special case, you use a separate file to track each person's or business's finances.)

In fact, to keep things perfectly clear, you should probably use the Activities⇨Create New Account command to open new accounts. That way, you won't run the risk of accidentally setting up a new file, something you very likely don't want to do.

How You Use It

When you choose the File⇨New command, Quicken displays a dialog box that asks, via a couple of cute radio buttons, whether you want to create a new account or a new file. You click one of the radio buttons and choose OK.

If you indicate you want a new file, Quicken displays another dialog box that asks for the name of the file and a directory location. (If you don't understand how filenames and directories work, you shouldn't be noodling around with new file creation just yet. You'll need to learn about file naming and hard disk organization first.)

Finally, Quicken displays a third window, the Create New Account window, that you use to create an account or two for the new file.

If you indicate that you want a new account in the aptly named Creating new file: Are you sure? dialog box, Quicken takes you straight to the Create New Account window. There, you can tell Quicken the type of account you want: checking, savings, credit card, cash, money market, investment, asset, or liability. You click the button that corresponds to your choice and then, almost magically, Quicken displays EasyStep to walk you through the process of setting up a new account.

Steps

❶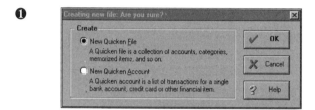

❷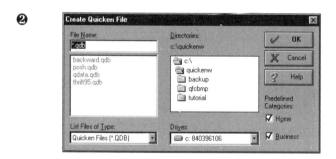

❸

More Stuff

Quicken automatically creates your first file, so most people who use Quicken won't ever need to worry about the Quicken file.

If you create a liability or an investment account, you need to provide more account information than an account name, description, balance, and starting date. In the case of a loan, for example, you need to tell Quicken how to calculate loan payments and how to apply the principal portions of these payments to the loan balance. In the case of an investment account, you need to tell Quicken which securities (the names of the stocks and bonds, for example) you've invested in.

TIP Maybe the fastest way to open a new account (besides choosing Activities⇨Create New Account) is to click Accts, click New and choose the kind of account you want to open.

File⇨Open

You use the File⇨Open command to flip-flop between the files you've created in Quicken. This means that you won't use this command until and unless you've already used the File⇨New command to create a new file.

How You Use It

When you choose this command, Quicken displays a dialog box that asks for the name of the file and a directory location. Use the Directories list box to give the file location. Use the File Name box to identify the file.

As I noted in the previous command entry, if you don't understand how filenames and directories work, you shouldn't be noodling around with multiple files.

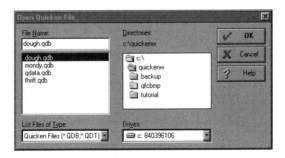

More Stuff

If you do start fooling around with this command, you may as well know that what Quicken calls a file is actually a set of files that all use the same filename but different file extensions. If this last statement sounds like Greek to you, don't worry. Just don't start creating new files.

Near the bottom of the File menu, right above the Exit command, is a list of the last four Quicken files you opened. If you want to open one these four, just click it.

File⇨File Operations⇨Copy

The File⇨File Operations⇨Copy command creates a second copy of a Quicken data file. As part of the copying process, you can specify that only transactions falling between certain dates should be copied. You can also choose a new location for the new file.

In general, there's only one good reason to use this command: Your Quicken data files have gotten too big for their own good. Maybe you're running out of memory, for example. Maybe you're having a terrible time backing up the files to a floppy disk. Or maybe Quicken seems very, v-e-r-y s-l-o-w.

How You Use It

When you choose this command, Quicken displays a dialog box that asks for the name of the new Quicken file and a directory location. Be sure to choose a meaningful name so you can tell what's in the file if you ever need to fool with it. The name can be up to eight characters long. It can't include the following characters: / ? : * " < > |.

The dialog box also asks for the range of dates in which transactions should fall to be included in the new file and whether old uncleared transactions and old investment transactions should be included — even if they fall before the start of the transaction dates range.

In 99 out of 100 cases, you will want to include the old uncleared transactions and the old investment transactions. Most people, therefore, should leave the Copy All Prior Uncleared Transactions (and the Copy All Prior Investment Transactions if you have an investment account in the file) check boxes marked.

When the Copy operation finishes, Quicken displays a message box telling you so.

Steps

❶
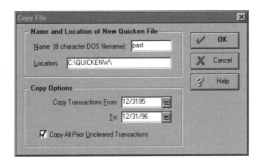

❷

More Stuff

You'll want to keep the financial records for a year in the same file. Therefore, the starting date for the transaction range should always be the first day of the year.

File⇨File Operations⇨Delete

The File⇨File Operations⇨Delete command erases a Quicken file. The Quicken file stores all your financial records, so erasing the Quicken file is functionally equivalent to burning up all your financial records in a backyard bonfire. Accordingly, you probably won't ever want to use this command. And if you do use it, make a backup copy of the file you're going to delete (using File⇨Backup) before you delete it. That way, you'll have something to fall back on if you regret your decision to delete your records.

How You Use It

When you choose this command, Quicken displays a dialog box that asks for the name of the file and a directory location. Use the Directories list box to give the file location. Use the File Name box to identify the file.

When you've correctly identified the file you want to destroy, choose OK. Quicken, surprised you're really trying to delete a file, displays a dialog box that asks you, in effect, "Really?" You type the word **yes** in the space provided and click OK.

Steps

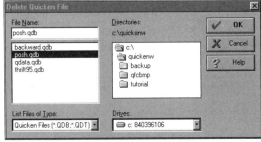

More Stuff

What Quicken calls a file is actually a collection of files that use the same filename but different file extensions. So, when you delete a Quicken file, you actually erase a bunch of different files.

I don't want to raise false hopes, but there's something you should know. It may be possible to unerase a previously erased file.

To do this in Windows 3.x, you can use the DOS undelete command or the Windows Undelete utility. In Windows 95, you open the Recycle Bin, click the file you want back, and choose File⇨Restore. How you use these tools is beyond the scope of this book. You'll need to refer to your Windows 95 user documentation, or you'll need to look up these commands in *Windows 95 For Dummies* or another such reference book.

File ⟹ File Operations ⟹ Rename

The File⟹File Operations⟹Rename command lets you change the name of a Quicken file.

How You Use It

When you choose this command, Quicken displays a dialog box that asks for the name and the directory location of the file you want to rename. Use the Directories list box to give the file location. Use the File Name box to identify the file.

When you've correctly identified the file you want to rename, enter the new name in the New Name for Quicken File text box. Can't find that box? It's in the lower right corner of the Rename Quicken File dialog box.

A filename must be eight or fewer characters long, and it can't include the following characters: / ? : * " < > | .When you've typed in the name, click OK.

 If you don't know what to name the file, here are my ideas: Newt (short for Newton), Beavis (after the MTV idiot), and Alex (one of the unisex names that in the '90s can be used for both girls and boys). All of my suggested names, by the way, follow DOS file-naming conventions. Yours will need to, too.

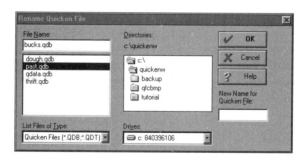

More Stuff

In the lower left corner of the Rename Quicken File dialog box, you find a List Files of Type drop-down list box. Don't worry about this. It's meaningless and doesn't do anything at all. What Quicken calls a file is actually a collection of files that use the same filename but different file extensions. When you rename a Quicken file, you actually rename a bunch of different files — not just those of a certain type or just those with a particular (or peculiar) filename.

File➪_File Operations_➪_Validate_

The File➪File Operations➪Validate command tells Quicken to look over your data and make sure that everything is intact. Basically, what this command does is make sure that the transactions in your registers, the categories in your category list, and just about all your other financial information work as they ought to work.

How You Use It

When you choose this command, Quicken shows you a dialog box with all your Quicken files in it. Choose the one you want to validate and click OK. Quicken gets right to work and does the job. And that's all there is to it. You see a dialog box with the message: `Quicken has validated your file and found no data losses.`

 Choose File➪File Operations➪Validate if you think something is amiss with your financial data. The Validate command rebuilds your data file, if that turns out to be necessary.

File➪_Year-End Copy_

You use the File➪Year-End Copy command to create archive copies of a chunk of transactions — such as only last year's transactions. You can also use this command to move old, unneeded transactions out of the file you work with and into another storage file.

How You Use It

When you choose this command, Quicken displays a dialog box, cleverly named the Year-End Copy dialog box, that asks whether you want to create an Archive copy of the file or a Start New Year copy of the file. (The Start New Year option is the one you use to move old transactions to a storage file.) Indicate your choice with a mouse click and then choose OK.

If you tell Quicken you want to archive, Quicken next displays a dialog box that asks for the archive filename, the archive file location, and the cutoff that determines whether a transaction goes into the archive file. (Transactions with dates on or before the cutoff date go into the archive file.) You make your choices — after much thought of course — and then you choose OK. _Voilà_. You're done.

Quicken, now a bit confused, doesn't know which file it should
use: the current file (which you used to create the archive file) or
the archive file (the file you just created, like, a sentence ago). So,
it displays another message box to ask you which one you want.
Again, a mouse click is in order. You click the option button that
corresponds to the file you want to use. Then you click OK.

Steps

❶

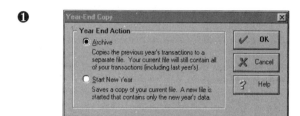

❷

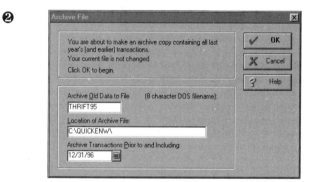

❸

If you tell Quicken that you want to start a new year, Quicken
displays the Start New Year dialog box, which lets you strip out all
of the old transactions from the current file. (An "old" transaction
is any cleared, noninvestment transaction that falls before the

cutoff date you specify.) With the Start New Year dialog box, you name the storage file Quicken creates for all your old transactions, and, optionally, you specify a file location. You also indicate a cutoff date. Then you choose OK.

Quicken first makes a copy of the file using the specified filename and directory location; then it deletes the old transactions in the existing file — the one you're working with — so that it's smaller and more manageable.

Steps

❶
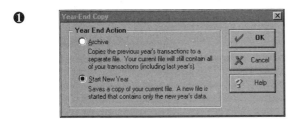

❷
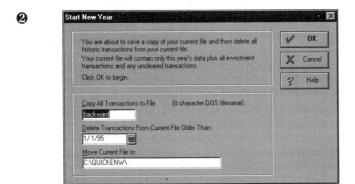

About April 15 every year, use the File⇨Year-End Copy command and the Start New Year option to clean up your Quicken file. To do this, use December 31 as a cutoff. All of the previous year's transactions will get copied into a storage file and then deleted from the current file. (The current file is the one you work with.)

File⇨Passwords⇨File

The File⇨Passwords⇨File command lets you create a file password that you or anyone else needs to supply before opening the Quicken file. If you've assigned a password to the last file you worked with, for example, Quicken asks for the file password immediately after you start the program. (Quicken automatically opens the Quicken file you worked with last.) If you can't supply the password, you won't be able to see or work with the Quicken file.

Remember, the Quicken file is the storage container that holds all your financial information. You definitely want to be able to work with this file, so choose passwords, and use passwords, carefully.

Although all this super-secrecy stuff may sound neat to Tom Clancy fans, there's a problem with passwords, darn it. You've got to remember them. If you forget your password, it's the same thing as erasing your Quicken file.

How You Use It

When you choose this command, Quicken displays the Set Up Password dialog box. To use this dialog box, first look over your shoulder to make sure that someone isn't watching. If the coast is clear, enter a password into the Password text box. Quicken doesn't display the characters you type; as an extra security precaution, it displays asterisks instead. (This is why the really nefarious types — your typical archcriminal, for example — watch the keys you press and not the screen.)

Just to make sure that you know what you've typed, you have to type your password all over again in the Confirm Password text box. You enter the password a second time to prove to Quicken that you know what you typed the first time. Once you've entered the password the same way twice, choose OK.

The next time someone tries to open this Quicken file, that someone will need to supply the password in the Quicken Password dialog box.

Steps

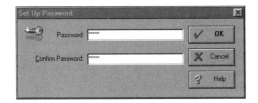

More Stuff

To change a file password, you also use the File⇨Passwords⇨File command. If you've set up a password already, Quicken displays the Change Password dialog box when you choose this command. You enter the existing password, enter the new password, and then confirm you know what you entered as the new password.

To get rid of a password, you also use the File⇨Passwords⇨File command. This time, however, you specify the new password as a blank. That's right, a blank. You don't enter anything into the New Password text box.

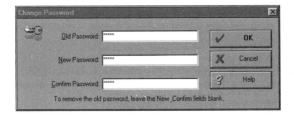

Oh, wait a minute. Here are a couple more things you should maybe know. First, a password can have up to 16 characters. Second, Quicken doesn't distinguish between uppercase and lowercase characters. In other words, it doesn't matter if your password is OpenSesame or oPENsESAME. All you have to do is get the letters right.

File⇨Passwords⇨Transaction

The File⇨Passwords⇨Transaction command lets you create a transaction password that you or anyone else needs to supply before editing existing (already entered) transactions that fall before a cutoff date.

Most people won't need to use this command, but I can think of one situation when it can come in handy. If you're in a business and you want a way to make sure that someone can't change last month's or last year's records, you can use a transaction password to effectively "lock up" transactions that shouldn't be changed.

How You Use It

When you choose the File⇨Passwords⇨Transactions command, Quicken displays the Password to Modify Existing Transactions dialog box. If the coast is clear, enter a password into the Password text box. Quicken displays asterisks instead of the characters you type in case any shady characters are looking over your shoulder. To make sure that you know exactly what you're typing in, you have to type the password a second time in the Confirm Password text box. Finally, enter the cutoff date.

From now on, anytime someone tries to change a transaction with a date falling on or before the cutoff date, he, she, or it will have to supply the transaction password you've just given.

Steps

❶

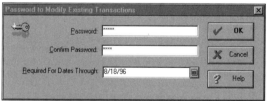

❷

More Stuff

To change a transaction password, you use the File⇨Passwords⇨Transaction command (a big surprise to you, no doubt). If you've set up a transaction password already, Quicken displays the Change Transaction Password dialog box when you choose this command. You enter the existing password, enter the new password, and then confirm that you know what you entered as the new password.

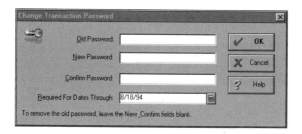

To get rid of a password, you also use the File⇨Passwords⇨Transaction command, but you specify the new password as a blank. To do this, you just don't enter anything into the New Password text box.

By the way, as with file passwords, a transaction password can be up to 16 characters long. What's more, Quicken doesn't distinguish between uppercase and lowercase characters, so it doesn't matter if you enter alacazam or ALACAZAM as the password, because both will do the trick.

File⇨Backup

The File⇨Backup command makes a copy of a Quicken file. If something bad happens to the Quicken file on your hard disk, you can use this backup copy to start over.

You should back up your Quicken files. You really and truly should. In fact, if you enter a lot of data in the program and you try to exit without backing up your file, Quicken puts a dialog box on-screen that tells you how important it is to back up data and gives you the opportunity to do it.

How You Use It

When you choose the File⇨Backup command, Quicken displays a
dialog box that asks whether you want to back up the current
file — the one you're already working with — or some other file. If
you choose to back up some other file, you have to select the file
from a list Quicken displays.

The dialog box also provides a drop-down list box for you to select
which floppy drive you want to send the file to: A, B, and so on.
When you've identified the file and the floppy drive, choose OK.

Quicken backs up the file you have chosen. When it finishes, it
displays a message that tells you whether it's been successful in
backing up your file.

Steps

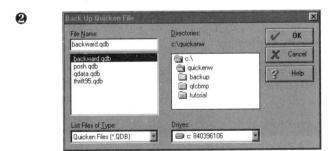

More Stuff

You should make it a practice to back up your Quicken data whenever you finish working. But in case you don't do that, Quicken reminds you when you need to back up your files. Every once in a while when you exit the program, you see the Automatic Backup dialog box. It tells you that you haven't backed up your files lately and gives you a golden opportunity to do so. Just put a disk in the A or B drive and choose Backup.

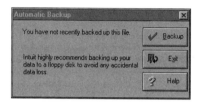

If the Quicken file you want to back up is too large to fit on a single floppy disk, Quicken displays a message box that alerts you. In this case, you can try another floppy disk — perhaps one that is larger or has more available space. Or you can choose to back up the file onto several disks.

So what happens if your Quicken data got mangled and you need to use the data on the backup copy? In that case, my friend, you should read the next entry in this book, "File⇨Restore."

One interesting and semisecret feature of Quicken is this: Quicken creates a backup copy of the Quicken file all on its own and stores this backup file in a BACKUP subdirectory in the Quicken directory. If your hard disk fails or some miscreant steals your PC, this backup copy isn't going to do you much good. But, if something bad happens to the actual working file or to the part of the hard disk where the actual working file is stored, this hidden backup copy of the Quicken file may just save your butt.

File⇨Restore

The File⇨Restore command copies the backup copy of a Quicken file stored on a floppy disk (or more than one floppy disk) onto your hard disk. So, if something happens to the Quicken file stored on your hard disk, you may be able to use the File⇨Restore command to recover most or all of your financial records data.

How You Use It

When you choose the File⇨Restore command, Quicken displays the Restore Quicken File dialog box. You might not know it, but this dialog box is asking for the name and location of the backup Quicken file copy you want to restore to your hard disk.

Chances are, the backup file is on a floppy disk you already put in the A or B drive. If that's the case, Quicken has already selected the backup file for you. But if that isn't so, use the Directories list box to give the backup copy file location and use the File Name box to identify the backup copy file. When you've correctly identified the file, choose OK. Quicken restores the file. When it finishes, it displays another message box.

Steps

❶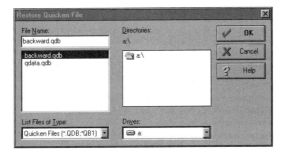

❷

More Stuff

If you didn't create a floppy disk backup, you may want to try restoring the Quicken file by using the backup file in the BACKUP subdirectory in the Quicken directory.

After you restore a Quicken file from a backup copy, you need to reenter any transactions you entered since the backup copy was made. If you printed copies of the Account Register, you can use this printout to see what transactions are missing from the newly restored file. If you didn't print copies, hmmm, well, I guess you can use old bank statements or old checkbook records, or just try your memory.

File⇨_Import_

You use the _File_⇨_Import_ command to take transactions stored in a QIF file and plop them into a Quicken file. This procedure isn't all that easy. It's rife with opportunities to wildly foul up your data. And it's something that — at least in my experience — only the truly foolish and the very young should attempt.

Let me tell you two more things about QIF files. First, a QIF file is a file that follows the Quicken Interchange Format — hence the acronym-derived name, QIF. Second, QIF rhymes with "sniff."

How You Use It

When you choose this command, Quicken displays a dialog box that asks for the pathname of the QIF file you want to import. If you don't know where the file is — and you probably don't know for sure — click the Browse button to display the Import from QIF File dialog box. Then use it to locate the QIF file.

The dialog box also provides a drop-down list so you can tell Quicken which account to plop the QIF file transactions into. It also provides check boxes to say what kind of stuff from the QIF file should be plopped: just transactions, transactions and accounts, categories, and so on.

If you click OK a couple of times — once on the Import from QIF File dialog box and once on the Import QIF dialog box — Quicken diligently begins work. When it finishes, Quicken displays a message box.

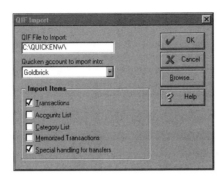

More Stuff

If you're moving data from one checkbook program to another —
say from Quicken to Microsoft Money or vice versa — you do so
with QIF files.

File➪Export

You use the File➪Export command to take transactions stored in
a Quicken file and plop them into a QIF file. A QIF file is a file that
follows the Quicken Interchange Format (see preceding entry).

Why you would want this QIF file or what you would do with it is
a mystery to me. The only time I can think you'd use this utility is
if you decide you don't want to use Quicken anymore, and so you
move to another checkbook program (such as Microsoft Money).

How You Use It

When you choose this command, Quicken displays a dialog box
that asks for the pathname of the QIF file you want to export. The
dialog box also provides a drop-down list box you use to specify
from which account the transactions should be exported, and
check boxes for specifying what kind of stuff should be exported:
just transactions, transactions and accounts, categories, and so on.

If you can't remember the path of the QIF file you want to export,
click the Browse button, root around until you find the file, and
click it.

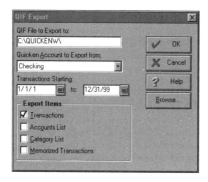

More Stuff

If you've just read the File Import command entry and are thinking to yourself, "Hmmm. This sounds familiar," you're right. The QIF Import and QIF Export dialog boxes and mechanics closely resemble each other.

File ⇨ *Save* *Desktop*

You use the File⇨Save Desktop command to tell Quicken when it should save the desktop. "Save the desktop" sounds kind of ominous, as if the desktop is an endangered species.

Actually, the *desktop* is just the application window in which all the Quicken document windows are arranged. With the File⇨Save Desktop command, you can tell Quicken what you want to see when you start the program.

How You Use It

When you choose this command, Quicken displays a dialog box that gives you two choices: Save Desktop on Exit and Save Current Desktop. If you click the first choice, Quicken brings you to whatever you were doing last each time you start the program. In other words, if you were in the Checking Register when you closed Quicken, you will see the Checking Register the next time you open the program.

If you click Save Current Desktop, Quicken shows you what's currently on the screen each time you start the program. In other words, the next time you start the program, you see what was on the screen when you chose Save Current Desktop.

More Stuff

The File⇨Save Desktop command is a neat way speed up your work with Quicken. If you use the Write Checks window most often, for example, you can have Quicken open directly to the Write Checks window. Or, if you just want to pick up where you left off each time you start Quicken, you can choose the Save Desktop on Exit option.

File⇨Printer Setup⇨Report/Graph Printer Setup

The File⇨Printer Setup⇨Report/Graph Printer Setup command lets you noodle around with the way the Windows printer setup affects reports and graphs. And all from within Quicken. (Gee whiz.)

You can use this command, for example, to change the active Windows printer used for report and graph printing, change page margins on reports and graphs, and adjust the fonts used in the things you print.

How You Use It

When you choose this command, Quicken displays the Report Printer Setup dialog box. It provides drop-down list boxes you use to change the printer settings, text boxes you use to specify margin sizes, and a couple of command buttons you use to display additional dialog boxes for making font changes.

You need to be careful if you make changes in the Report Printer Setup dialog box. For example, if you change the active printer but that printer is really not active (or even available), your Quicken reports and graphs won't print. Or, if you create monstrously large margins, your reports may look funny or may not fit on the page.

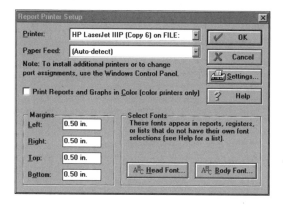

More Stuff

The Report Printer Setup dialog box also provides a Settings command button. You can click this button to access the other Windows printer setup settings, such as page orientation, paper tray source, paper size, number of copies, and so on.

File⇨Printer Setup⇨Check Printer Setup

The File⇨Printer Setup⇨Check Printer Setup command lets you noodle around with the way the Windows printer setup affects check printing. You can use this command to change the active Windows printer used for check printing, change the check-form style, and tell Quicken when you want to print a partial page of checks.

How You Use It

When you choose this command, Quicken displays the Check Printer Setup dialog box. It provides drop-down list boxes you use to change the printer settings and check-form style and buttons you use to indicate how partial pages of check forms will be fed into the printer.

As with the Report/Graph Printer Setup command, you need to be careful here. If you make goofy changes, you'll end up with goofy-looking — and probably useless — checks.

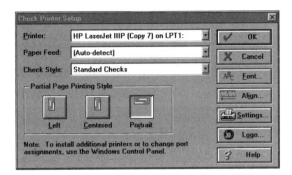

More Stuff

The Check Printer Setup dialog box provides several useful command buttons that give you additional control over how checks print.

- The Font command button lets you change the typeface and style as well as the font point size of letters and numbers on your checks.

- The Align command button lets you test and correct check-form alignment.

- The Settings command button gives you access to the other Windows printer setup settings, such as resolution, printer memory, page orientation, number of copies, and so on.

- The Logo command button lets you add a picture to checks (as long as you've got the picture stored as a bitmap image someplace on your hard disk).

File⇨Print Checks

You know what this command does, of course. It prints the checks.

How You Use It

To use this command, first you enter all the checks you want to print using the Write Checks window. Once you've got this done, you choose this command. (You can also click the Print button if the Write Checks window is displayed.)

Quicken next displays the Select Checks to Print dialog box, which you use to indicate which check number Quicken should print on the first check and whether you want to print all the checks you entered or just some of them.

The options on the Select Checks to Print dialog box depend on what kind of printer you have. For example, if you have a laser printer, Quicken wants to know how many checks are on each page of check forms — three, two, or one. It also needs to know which check style you want to print.

When you're ready to start printing, click OK.

When Quicken finishes printing the check or checks, it displays a message asking whether the checks printed okay. If they did, choose OK. If one or more checks didn't print okay, enter the check number of the first check that didn't print correctly. In this case, Quicken lets you walk through the steps for printing those checks again.

Steps

❶

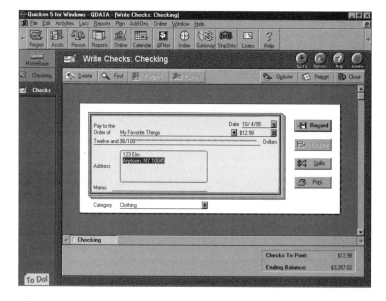

❷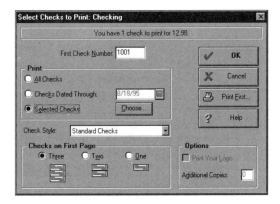

❸

More Stuff

If you want to print just some of the checks, you've got two routes
to go. When Quicken displays the Select Checks to Print dialog
box, you can mark the Checks Dated Through option button and
then enter a date in the text box provided. (In this case, as you've
undoubtedly figured out, Quicken only prints checks with dates
falling on or before the specified date.) Or you can mark the
Selected Checks option button, select the Choose command
button, and then, when Quicken displays a list of the checks
patiently waiting to be printed, mark checks by using the mouse.

If you're not sure whether the checks are aligned correctly in your
printer or whether your checks will print correctly, click the Print
First button. Quicken then prints only the first check in the run so
that you can make sure that it comes out right. I certainly hope it
does.

File➪_Print Register_

The _File_➪Print Register command prints a list of the transactions in an account and the balance after each transaction. In effect, this report is equivalent to the paper register you keep (or kept) for your checkbook and were supposed to fill out but didn't in the grocery store checkout line when you wrote a check.

How You Use It

To use the _File_➪Print Register command, first display the Register window with the account for which you want a register. You can do this by clicking the Registr icon. Then choose the _File_➪Print Register command or click the Print button on the iconbar.

Quicken displays the Print Register dialog box. Use this dialog box to indicate the range of dates for which transactions should be included. If you're the creative sort, you can give the register a title, too. ("The Life and Times of Riley Brown," if Riley Brown is your name, for example.) After you've done this stuff, select Print.

Quicken next displays the Print Report dialog box. You can use this dialog box to do all sorts of fancy-schmancy things: export to Lotus 1-2-3 (or Microsoft Excel) worksheet files, create delimited ASCII files (Ooooh), print your register sideways in landscape orientation (Wow), and even affect printer quality and color with the Head and Body Font buttons.

If you just want to print a register, all you've got to do is click OK. Go on. Don't be afraid. Just do it, as they say in those obnoxious sneaker ads.

Steps

❶

❷

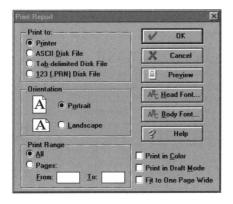

More Stuff

The Print Register dialog box that Quicken displays when you choose the File⇨Print Register command provides three check boxes that give you a bit of control over the way the printed register looks:

- You can use the Print One Transaction Per Line check box to tell Quicken that it should scrunch each transaction onto a single, hard-to-read line.

- You can use the Print Transaction Splits check box to tell Quicken that it should print any split information. (You should do this if you're using splits. Otherwise, you can't see how you've split amounts.)

- You can use the Sort By Check Number check box to force Quicken to arrange transactions by check number. (If you don't mark this check box, Quicken prints transactions in the same order you entered them.)

In the Print Report dialog box, use the Head Font and Body Font buttons to fool around with the typefaces and font sizes on the register, if you're so inclined. And if you are, be sure to click the Preview button before you print the register. You need to see what kind of a monster you've turned the register into before you send it through the printer.

File➪Exit

You use the File➪Exit command to close, or stop, the Quicken application and return to Windows. You should always use this command (or the Control menu's Close command) to close the Quicken application. Sure, exiting some other way — such as by turning off your computer — may be fun, faster, or emotionally satisfying. But you can damage pieces of the Quicken file if you don't close Quicken by using the File➪Exit command. (Fortunately, Quicken can almost always repair the damage.)

 When you exit Quicken, it checks to see whether you've recently backed up the Quicken file. If you haven't, Quicken displays a message that says you haven't recently backed up and asks if you want to do this. You can click the Backup button (which appears on the message box) to do a backup (just like the one described in the File➪Backup command entry). Or you can click the Exit button to indicate that you like living on the edge.

By the way, Quicken saves your data whenever you record a new transaction. You won't ever see one of those "Do you want to save your changes?" warning boxes that appear in other computer programs if you try to exit without saving the changes you've made to a file. No, siree. Why, you won't even find a Save command in Quicken.

Edit Menu Commands

Here's the short story on the Edit menu. The Edit menu's commands help you enter stuff into the Register and Write Checks windows. These commands also help you find and fix errors you may make while entering stuff into these windows. You don't need to use any of these commands to make good use of Quicken. But knowing a bit about the commands on the Edit menu can save you time.

Edit⇨Undo

Use the Edit⇨Undo command to undo the last edit to a transaction. In other words, use this command to reverse the effect of the edit or entry you just made.

How You Use It

Choose the Edit⇨Undo command after you've done something you really wish you hadn't.

By the way, if there's nothing to undo, Quicken disables this command. (To show the command is disabled, Quicken changes the color of the command name's letters to gray.)

More Stuff

You can only *undo*, or reverse, text editing in a field. You can't undo a bunch of changes — such as all the changes you've made to a record. This means, for instance, that you can't undo the Edit⇨Void Transaction, thereby "unvoiding" the transaction. And it means you can't undo the Edit⇨Delete Transaction command either.

 If you haven't yet recorded your changes to a transaction, and you regret having made your changes, you can click the Edit button in the Register window and choose Restore Transaction from the drop-down menu.

Perhaps, just perhaps, there's a lesson in all this. Maybe no one should rely on the Edit⇨Undo command but rather just remember that it's there. Because maybe, just maybe, it'll save you some trouble sometime.

Edit⇨Cut

Use the Edit⇨Cut command to move whatever you've selected in a text box to the Clipboard. The Clipboard is Window's temporary storage area. You usually store things on the Clipboard when you want to move them from one text box to another. This command is usually used with the Edit⇨Paste command.

How You Use It

To use the Edit⇨Cut command, select whatever you want to move. Then choose this command.

Selecting stuff is a Windows technique, so I'm not going to describe how you do it here in tedious detail. But I will give you a couple of tips.

- When you first move the selection cursor to a text box, Windows usually selects the text box contents. So, that's one way to select something you want to copy to the Clipboard.

- You can also select text box contents by dragging the mouse over whatever it is you want to select.

You'll know when something has been selected because it is highlighted on the screen.

More Stuff

When you move or copy something to the Clipboard, whatever is already stored on the Clipboard is replaced with the new stuff you've copied.

 All the Windows applications you've got running share the Clipboard. So, if you're running more than one application at once, something you've moved or copied to the Clipboard with one application (such as Quicken) will be replaced if you move or copy something else with another application (such as Lotus 1-2-3).

 One more thing to note is that, because the Clipboard is a Windows feature and not specific to Quicken, it's a convenient way to move stuff between Quicken and other applications — such as a word processor or spreadsheet application. To move something to the Clipboard, you almost always use the application's Edit⇨Cut or Edit⇨Copy command. To move something from the Clipboard to the current application, you almost always use the application's Edit⇨Paste command.

 *Edit⇨Copy*

Use the Edit⇨Copy command to copy whatever you've selected in a text box to the Clipboard, Window's temporary storage area. Note that the only difference between the Edit⇨Cut and Edit⇨Copy command is that, when you use Edit⇨Copy, you don't remove the selected text from the text box; you just duplicate it. This command is generally used with the Edit⇨Paste command.

How You Use It

To use this command, select whatever you want to copy. Then choose Edit⇨Copy.

More Stuff

I describe how to select stuff you want to cut in the Edit⇨Cut entry and talk a bit about some of the little nuances and subtleties of the Clipboard. If you've got the time, peruse the previous entry.

Edit⇨Paste

Use the Edit⇨Paste command to copy the contents of the Clipboard to the text box with the selection cursor. Typically, you use the Edit⇨Paste command with the Edit⇨Cut or Edit⇨Copy command to move stuff between text boxes. If you're a wild man (or wild woman), however, you can use the Edit⇨Cut, Edit⇨Copy, and Edit⇨Paste commands to move stuff between applications as well as text boxes.

How You Use It

To use the Edit⇨Paste command, move the selection cursor to the text box into which you want to put the Clipboard contents. Next, position the cursor at the exact location where the new stuff should be plopped. Then choose this command.

More Stuff

If you select stuff in a text box, choosing the Edit⇨Paste command tells Quicken to replace what you've selected with what's stored on the Clipboard. If you don't select stuff, choosing the Edit⇨Paste command just inserts what's stored on the Clipboard.

You don't change or lose the Clipboard contents when you paste. Whatever you've stored on the Clipboard just hangs around, like cigarette smoke. So you can reuse what you've stored on the Clipboard as many times as you want. Just keep choosing this command over and over again. When you copy something new to the Clipboard, however, what was there before is erased. The Clipboard can only hang onto one thing at a time.

Edit⇨New Transaction

You can use the Edit⇨New Transaction command to select the last row of the register and move the selection cursor to its first text box. You don't actually need to use the Edit⇨New command to do this, however. A mouse click works just as nicely. So do the arrow keys.

To insert a blank row in the middle of a register, use the Edit⇨Insert Transaction command.

How You Use It

To use this command, just choose Edit⇨New Transaction. Yep. That's all there is to it.

To actually enter the new transaction, of course, you have to type in dates, numbers, payee or payer names, and a category.

This command does have one fringe benefit: If you're at or near the top of a register with a lot of entries, and you want to get to the bottom of the register quickly to make a new entry, choose Edit⇨New Transaction. Quicken sends you straight to the bottom faster than lightning. (Another way to get to the bottom of a register quickly is to press Ctrl+End.)

By the way, if you want to get to a certain date in a register quickly, press Ctrl+G, enter a date in the Go To Date dialog box, and click OK.

Edit⇨Edit

(Is there an echo in here?) You can use the Edit⇨Edit command to make changes to the selected list entry.

How You Use It

To use the Edit⇨Edit command, you first need to display a list showing the thing you want to change. To change an account description, for example, you first display the Account List window by choosing the Lists⇨Account command or clicking the Accts icon. If you want to change the name of one of the accounts shown on the list, you select it and then choose the Edit⇨Edit Account command.

More Stuff

The Edit⇨Edit command doesn't apply to the Register window's rows. Nor does it apply to the Write Checks window. It applies only when you've displayed a list by using a Lists menu command.

One other thing. The exact name of the Edit⇨Edit command depends on the list displayed. If the Category & Transfer List shows, the command name is Edit⇨Edit Category. If the Account List shows, the command name is Edit⇨Edit Account.

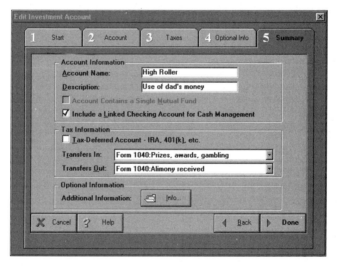

Edit⇨Delete

You can use the Edit⇨Delete command to remove a selected transaction in a Register window, remove a selected list entry, or erase a check shown in a Write Checks window.

How You Use It

To use the Edit⇨Delete command, select the thing you want to delete. Then choose this command. Quicken will probably display a message box that asks you to confirm your deletion. It might even ask you to type the word "yes."

Steps

 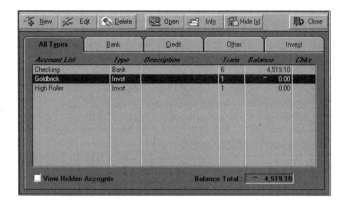

If you're thinking to yourself that this isn't exactly rocket science, you're right.

More Stuff

Like many of the Edit menu commands, the exact name of the Edit⇨Delete command depends on the thing that's displayed on your screen. If the thing displayed is a register, the command name is Edit⇨Delete Transaction. If the thing displayed is a list of categories, the command name is Edit⇨Delete Category. If it's a list of accounts . . . but you get the idea.

 Maybe the fastest way to delete a transaction in a register is to click the little Edit button and select Delete Transaction from the pull-down menu.

Edit⊅Insert Transaction

You can use the Edit⊅Insert Transaction command to insert a blank row in a register. You do this so that you can plop a transaction into the blank row created by this command.

How You Use It

To use the Edit⊅Insert Transaction command, select the transaction above which you want to insert a new transaction. Choose this command and then enter the transaction data into the new, empty row.

Steps

❶

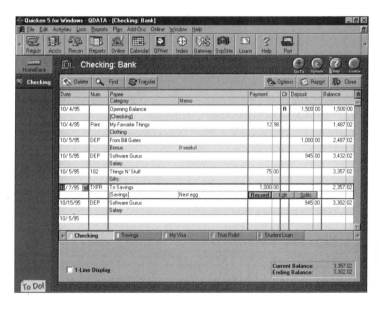

❷

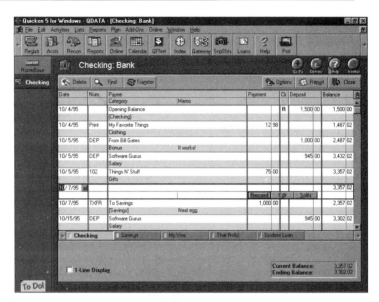

Edit⇨Void Transaction

Use the Edit⇨Void Transaction command to mark a transaction as one that shouldn't be included in the account balance or in any reports.

Typically, you use this command when you want to keep a record of a transaction's existence, but don't want the transaction included in calculations. For example, if you make a mistake writing out a check and then void the check (by scrawling the word *VOID* across the check), you could record your little mistake by entering a check into the register and voiding it. You might also void a check if you've stopped payment on it.

How You Use It

To use the Edit⇨Void Transaction command, select the transaction you want to void and choose this command. Quicken inserts the word VOID in front of the payee or payer name, sets the transaction amount as zero, and marks the check or deposits as cleared.

Steps

❶

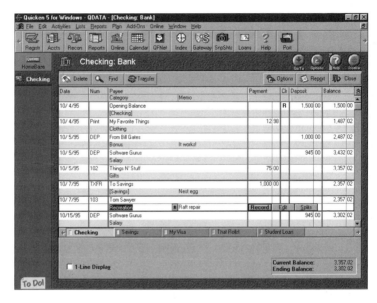

❷

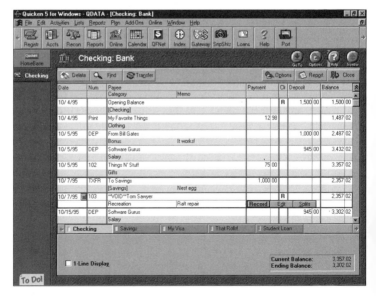

Edit⇨Copy Transaction

Use the Edit⇨Copy Transaction command to make a copy of the selected transaction. You do this when you want to later paste the copied transaction into another row of the register or into another account's register. You generally use this command with the Edit⇨Paste Transaction command.

How You Use It

To use the Edit⇨Copy Transaction command, click the mouse on (or press the up- or down-arrow key until you land on) the transaction you want to copy. Then choose this command. Quicken copies the transaction to a temporary storage area.

More Stuff

When Quicken copies a transaction, it doesn't copy it to the Clipboard. Quicken copies the transaction to a temporary storage area. I don't know what folks at Quicken call this storage area, so I call it the *transaction bucket.* (Sorry, I can't think of a better term.) Like the Clipboard, however, this temporary storage area stores only one item — in this case, one transaction — at a time. So the next time you use the Edit⇨Copy Transaction command, Quicken replaces what's already stored in the transaction bucket.

When you choose the Edit⇨Copy Transaction command, Quicken beeps not once, but three times. You could scare a cat that way.

Edit⇨Paste Transaction

Use the Edit⇨Paste Transaction command to copy the contents of the transaction bucket (a temporary storage area where things you've copied are held) into an empty row of the register. This command is generally used with the Edit⇨Copy Transaction command.

How You Use It

To use the Edit⇨Paste Transaction command, click the mouse on — or press the up- and down-arrow keys until you arrive at — the row where you want to paste the transaction you've already copied. Then choose this command.

More Stuff

WARNING! Be careful when using the Edit⇨Paste Transaction command. If you paste a transaction into a row that already has a transaction, you'll wipe out the old transaction with the new transaction.

Edit⇨Memorize Transaction

Using the Edit⇨Memorize Transaction command, you can memorize, or permanently store, transactions you will reuse time and time again.

This sounds kooky, but it's not. Really. Take the case of that monthly check you write to pay your mortgage or your rent. Most of the information you enter each month is the same. So, by storing this information that is the same month in and month out, you can save yourself scads of time. This command is generally used with the Lists⇨Memorized Transaction command.

How You Use It

To use the Edit⇨Memorize Transaction command, click the mouse on — or press the up- and down-arrow keys until you arrive at — the row with the transaction you want to memorize. Then, with one sure, swift, and fluid motion, choose the Edit⇨Memorize Transaction command. Finally, click OK.

More Stuff

Quicken automatically memorizes transactions unless you've told it to do otherwise by using the Edit⇨Options command. Yes, that's right. If Quicken is running the way it wants to, you should never have to use the Edit⇨Memorize Transaction command because the whole memorization thing is already going on. And right under your nose.

Quicken also automatically recalls transactions if what you're entering in the payee box looks familiar. Let's say, for example, that you (or Quicken) has previously memorized a $25 check to "Harley's House of Hops," the local beer-making supply store. If you begin typing the first few letters of the supply store's name, Quicken automatically fills in the rest of the payee box with "Harley's House of Hops." But it gets better. If you press the Tab key — Pepsi doesn't work, by the way — Quicken fills in the rest of the memorized transaction information: the check amount, any memo description you entered, and the category.

You can see a list of the transactions you've memorized by choosing the Lists➪Memorized Transactions command. And to think of the fun you'll have with that!

One more thing: If you don't want Quicken to memorize your transactions automatically, choose Edit➪Options, click the Checks button, click the QuickFill tab, and click the Automatic Memorization of New Transactions check box to uncheck it.

 And yet another thing: You can have Quicken remove memorized transactions from the transactions list after a period of months has elapsed. If you haven't written a check to somebody in, say, the last two months, you can have Quicken take that somebody off the transactions list automatically. Here's how: Select Edit➪Options, click the General button, put a check in the Remove memorized transactions used in last check box, and enter a **2** in the little box to the right that says Months.

The main reason for removing memorized transactions from the list is to keep the list from getting too long. Scrolling through a long list of transactions to get to the one you want defeats the purpose of memorizing transactions.

Edit➪Find/Replace

You can use the Edit➪Find/Replace command to make changes to a bunch of transactions at once. For example, if you've been misspelling some payee name, you could use the Edit➪Find/Replace command to correct the misspellings throughout a register.

How You Use It

To use the Edit➪Find/Replace command, first choose the command. Quicken then displays the Find and Replace dialog box.

Describe the transactions you're looking for by using the Find, Search, and Match if boxes. In the Find box, enter what it is you're looking for. If you're looking in a long register, make choices from the Search and Match if boxes, too (otherwise don't bother). Click the Search box and choose the column from the pull-down menu that the thing you're looking for is likely to be in. The Match if box is just another way to narrow a search. Take a look at the Match if choices and choose one, if you so desire.

Then select the Find All button. Quicken displays a list of the transactions that match your description. Next, describe which column in the found transactions you want to replace — the Amount, Cleared Status, Memo, Category/Class, Check Number, or Payee column. In the With text box, enter the text of the replacement. Then mark the transactions that you want to change by clicking in the left-hand column next to the transactions.

When you select Replace, Quicken displays a message box asking you to confirm your replacements and then, assuming you click Yes, it displays another message box telling you about the replacements it has made.

Steps

❶

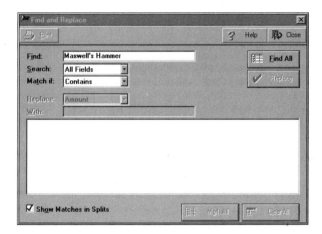

❷

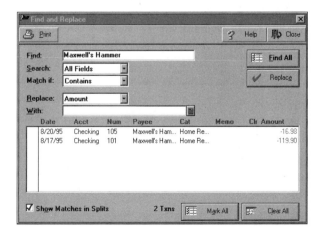

❸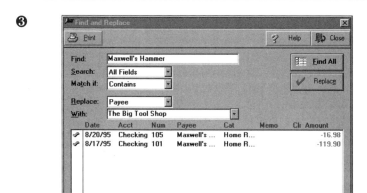

❹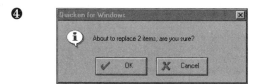

❺

More Stuff

If you intend to find and replace a whole bunch of data, make a
backup of your file (with File⇨Backup) before you do so. You
never quite know what a find and replace operation will do. It
might foul up your records in ways you didn't anticipate. If it
does, and you took my advice about making a backup, you can
select File⇨Restore to get your old data back.

Edit⇨Find

Use this command to describe a fragment of text or an amount you're looking for. Quicken takes the information you provide and searches high and low for a transaction that includes the text or amount.

How You Use It

To use the Edit⇨Find command, first choose the command (you can also choose it by clicking the Find button on a register). Quicken displays the Quicken Find dialog box, which provides a Find text box and two drop-down list boxes: Search and Match if.

In the Find text box, enter the text fragment or amount you want to locate. Use the Search drop-down list box to indicate which fields Quicken should search. (By default, Quicken looks at all the fields.) Use the Match if drop-down list box to indicate whether your entry should exactly match a field or only some portion of the field.

After you indicate what Quicken should look for and where it should look, click either the Find or the Find All command button. Click Find if you're just looking for one transaction. Click Find All if you know that a number of transactions match the Search and Match if criteria you described.

If you click Find, Quicken begins looking through the register for a transaction like the one described. If it finds one, it goes to the transaction in the register. That's all there is to it. If you want to do the search again, just click the Find button in the register and click Find in the dialog box again.

If you click Find All, your helpful friend Quicken displays a new, improved version of the Quicken Find dialog box that lists all the transactions that match your description. What if you want to look at just one of them? Good question. In that case, select the transaction you're interested in from the list by double-clicking on it. Quicken opens the register to the transaction you selected.

If you want to get back to the Quicken Find dialog box with all those transactions on it, click the Quicken Find QuickTab on the left side of your screen.

If Quicken can't find what you're looking for, a box comes on-screen that says, "No matching transactions were found." Better luck next time, kid.

Steps

❶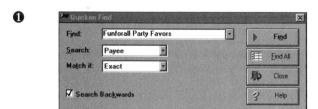

❷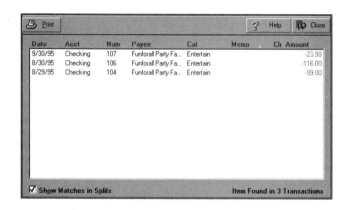

❸

More Stuff

You can use the Search Backwards check box to control which direction Quicken searches. If the check box isn't marked, Quicken looks at the subsequent transactions, starting from the selected transaction. If the check box is marked, Quicken looks at the previous transactions, starting with the selected transaction.

You can activate another window and search inside it by choosing one of the numbered Window menu commands. You can also reactivate the Find dialog box by choosing its QuickTab on the left side of the screen.

Edit⇨Go To Transfer

You can use this command to find out how, where, and when you made transfers between accounts. This command is invaluable if you have a number of accounts and you often transfer money between them. When you choose the Edit⇨Go To Transfer command, Quicken displays the other account's Register window and selects the transfer transaction.

How You Use It

To use the Edit⇨Go To Transfer command, select a transfer transaction, and choose the command.

For the obvious reason, this command doesn't work if the selected transaction isn't a transfer. It's just a neat way to go to another account and see where you transferred all that money.

Steps

❶

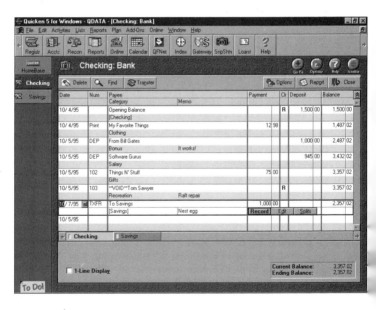

❷

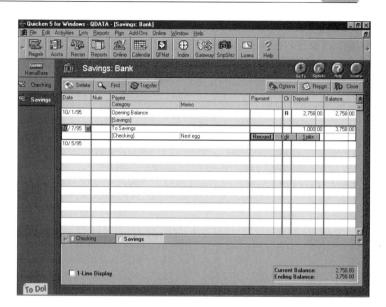

Edit▷Options

Quicken, as it's installed right out of the box, works mighty fine. Mighty fine, indeed. But if you're the sort of person who has to do it your way, know this: The Edit▷Options command lets you change the way Quicken works.

For example, you can tell Quicken that it should or shouldn't remind you to enter a category. And you can tell Quicken to at least attempt to guess what payee or payer name you're typing.

How You Use It

To use the Edit▷Options command, choose it. (If you're the speedy type, you can choose this command directly by clicking the Options button on the iconbar.) Quicken displays the Options window with a bunch of buttons: General, Checks, Register, Reports, Reminders, and Iconbar. Each button represents a set of settings. ("A set of settings," you say. "Sheesh. That doesn't make a whole lot of sense.")

For example, the General button, if clicked, displays a bunch of buttons you can click to change the way Quicken works. You make your choices, click OK to redisplay the Options dialog box, and then click Close.

Of course, if you're just starting to knock around with Quicken, you aren't going to have much of a clue as to what a "General" setting is. Which raises an important point. Fiddle-faddling with the Options settings isn't something you should do until you know a bit more about Quicken. Think of it this way: How can you know what you like until you figure out how to use what you've got?

More Stuff

Throughout this book, I give you advice about when you might want to change options with Edit⇨Options. The options found here pertain to almost everything you can do with Quicken. For the playful among you, here's a little rundown of some of the most important options.

My favorite option in the General Options dialog box is Use Bold Text in Dialogs. Put a check mark next to it if, like me, all this staring at computer screens is wearing out your eyeballs. This option makes it easier to read dialog boxes.

Notice the last check box on the top, the one called Remove Memorized Transactions...? Put a check in this box and enter a 1, 2, or 3 in the months box, and Quicken removes items from the memorized transaction list after the number of months you specify.

The Check Options dialog box has three tabs — Checks, Miscellaneous, and QuickFill. On the Checks tab, you may be interested in the first check box, which puts another field on your checks so you can write messages to payees or to yourself. There's also a check box for dating checks on the day they are printed, not the day they are recorded or entered.

Steps

❶

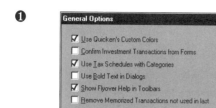

❷

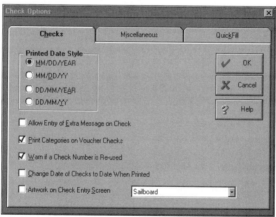

If you're a stickler for categorizing all your transactions, click
Warn Before Recording Uncategorized Transactions on the
Miscellaneous tab. That way, you'll never enter a transaction
without categorizing it in some way.

As you've probably noticed by now, Quicken memorizes transactions automatically. If you don't want it to do that, click the first
check box on the QuickFill tab to remove the check mark. Now,
when you want to memorize a transaction, you have to select it
and choose Edit↝Memorize Transaction.

The Register Options dialog box also has three tabs — Display, Miscellaneous, and QuickFill. Miscellaneous and QuickFill work pretty much like the tabs of the same name in the Check Options dialog box. Use the options on the Display tab to fiddle with the look of the register. You can even fool around with fonts and colors if you're the creative type.

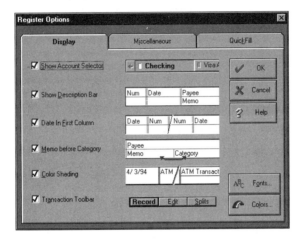

The main things of interest in the Report Options dialog box are the date ranges. You can change the time period that Quicken uses to gather data for its default reports with these date range options.

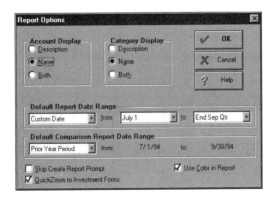

If you click the Reminders button, you get the Reminder Options dialog box, where you can turn on the Billminder. This little gizmo reminds you when it's time to pay bills or make transactions of one kind or another. (See the Activities⇨Reminders entry if you want to know more about this feature.)

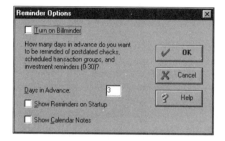

Click the Iconbar button to see the Customize Iconbar dialog box. From here you can change what the iconbar looks like and even change the order of icons on the bar. Shoot, you can even take icons off the bar if you want to.

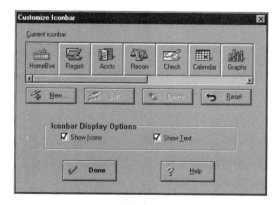

Activities Menu Commands

The Activities menu commands are hard to categorize. They do a bunch of different things: They let you flip-flop between windows, they let you set up budgets and loans, and they let you set up and use the CheckFree electronic payment service.

Perhaps — and I really think this is a good idea — the menu name should be potpourri? In fact, if you want to start a letter-writing campaign to try and convince Intuit that it should change the name, count me in.

Activities⇨Homebase

The Quicken HomeBase window, which is what appears when you choose the Activities⇨Homebase command, provides an alternative to the regular ol' Windows menu bar.

How You Use It

To open the Quicken HomeBase window, just choose this command or click the leftmost icon on the iconbar.

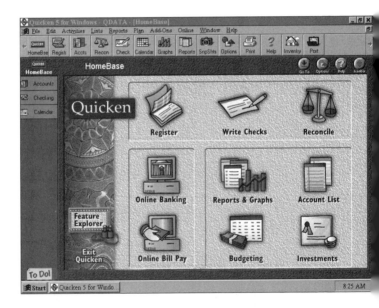

More Stuff

If you want it to, the HomeBase window can, in effect, become an alternative to the standard menu bar and menu system. Just start here instead of on the menu bar or iconbar when you want to use Quicken. To get to the HomeBase window quickly, all you have to do is click the HomeBase QuickTab on the left side of the screen.

That's some graphic on the HomeBase window, isn't it? If you look closely, you'll see scales, moneybags, rainbow-colored reinforcing rods, and even somebody's lost wallet. And if you stare at the hand long enough — the one that's holding the cash — it will swing around, reach out of your computer screen, and hand you the money. No lie! If you click the Exit Quicken sign in the lower left corner . . . well, see for yourself.

 I've found the last button on the HomeBase window, the Feature Explorer, very helpful for learning Quicken. You might, too. When you click the Feature Explorer button, a dialog box appears with a bunch of different topics. Click the one you're interested in to "explore" it.

Activities⇨Create New Account

You can guess what this command does, right? You choose Activities⇨Create New Account, and Quicken displays the dialog boxes you fill in to describe a new account you need.

How You Use It

Choose this command. Almost immediately, Quicken displays the Create New Account dialog box, which provides about half a dozen buttons to represent the different account types. To start, you just click one of the buttons — the one that corresponds to the account type you want.

Quicken next displays an Account Setup dialog box. The dialog box has several tabs, all of which you fill out to give the account's name, give the account's starting balance, enter the date you'll begin your record-keeping, sign up for online services, and (optional) describe the account.

Steps

❶

❷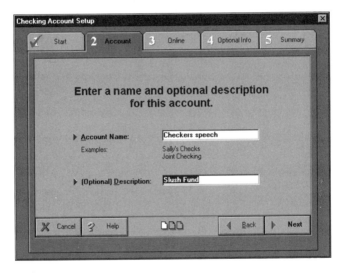

More Stuff

When you create bank accounts, money market accounts, cash accounts, and other asset accounts, your work is pretty simple. Provide a name, balance, and date, and you're done. If you want to get a little wild and crazy, you can provide a description. But still, the whole account-creation process is easy. Real easy.

In the case of a liability account, credit-card, or investment account, the process gets a bit more tricky. A credit card, for example, has a credit limit. In the case of a liability account, Quicken asks about the loan's payments, interest rate, and term so that it can make the principal amortization calculations. And, in the case of an investment account, well, let's just say you can't do this with your eyes closed and one arm tied behind your back. No way. Investment accounts are complicated.

If you want to set up one of the other, more complicated accounts, you probably need to feel comfortable winging it. You can't really get into any trouble doing this. The worst thing that can happen is you screw up and add a goofy account that you can't use, or you need to find the Quicken user documentation, get a friend, or yet another book to help.

While I'm on the subject of creating accounts, I should mention one other thing. Each of the Account Setup dialog boxes that Quicken displays also provides a tax-deferred account option. You can mark the Yes option button if you want to tell Quicken that any income the account produces — such as interest on a bank account — isn't taxed.

You probably won't have to worry about the tax-deferred business very often. About the only accounts that are tax deferred are retirement accounts: IRAs (Individual Retirement Accounts), Keoghs, SEP Plans (Simplified Employee Pension Plans), 401(k)s, and 403(b)s.

Activities⇨Write Checks

The Activities⇨Write Checks command opens the Write Checks window so that you can describe a check you want to print. You can also click the Check button on the iconbar to open the same window. Because clicking the Check button once is easier than clicking twice for the menu command, you'll probably never use this command. Never.

How You Use It

Just do it, as that obnoxious sneaker ad says. And when you have done it, you see the Write Checks window.

When you fill out a check in the Write Checks window, you can't enter a check number. The check you write appears in the register with the word "Print" in the Num box.

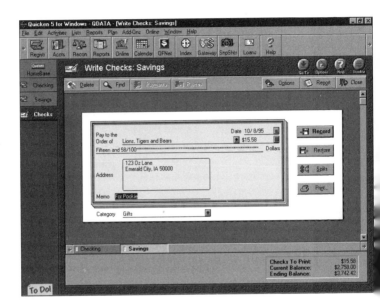

More Stuff

I don't have much more to say about the Activities⇨Write Checks command. But I'm suffering because my editor says I'm supposed to fill up a "More Stuff" section for each and every command. Hmmm. Hey, I know. Here's a totally unrelated but interesting tidbit I can tell you. People spend more on postage entering those sweepstakes-by-mail contests than the contest sponsors give away. Weird, huh?

Activities⇨Use Register

The Activities⇨Use Register command opens the Register window for the active account so that you can record checks and deposits into the Account Register. You can also click the Registr iconbar button to open the same window. So this command, like the one described in the preceding entry, is probably one that only masochists and the mouseless will use.

How You Use It

Choose this command or click its equivalent, the Registr iconbar
button, to see the register in all its glory.

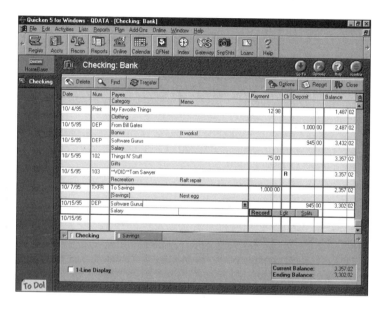

More Stuff

Here's a little nugget of knowledge that's sort of tangentially
related to this and the preceding command entry. You don't
actually have to use the Write Checks window to describe the
checks you want to print. You can use the Register window. The
only trick is that the Num field needs to be filled with the word
"Print." The word "Print," as you've already guessed, tells Quicken
to print the check.

In fact, and you probably saw this coming a mile away, when you
describe a check you want to print using the Write Checks
window, what Quicken actually does is enter a check into the
register and set the Num box to "Print."

I should mention one potential disadvantage of using the Register
window for describing checks to be printed. You don't have
anyplace to enter the address. So if you need to enter the
address — perhaps you're using windowed envelopes to mail
the checks — you need to use the Write Checks window.

Now you know the sort of challenges and dilemmas that, because I'm an accountant, fill my days. Should I or should I not use windowed envelopes? Hmmm.

Activities⇨Get Online Data

If you've signed up for Quicken's QuickBanking service, you can click this command to get up-to-date information about your financial status — that is, how many of your checks have cleared and that kind of thing.

Unfortunately, this little book doesn't have enough space to cover the online services in detail. Suffice it to say, you must have signed on with the service and you must have a modem connection to use this command.

Activities⇨Reconcile

You use the Activities⇨Reconcile command to *reconcile,* or balance, bank accounts and credit-card accounts. Before you quickly flip the page and pretend that you didn't just read the preceding sentence, let me tell you something. Reconciling a bank account or credit-card account in Quicken takes about two minutes. That's no joke. Two minutes.

How You Use It

Display the Register window for the bank account or credit-card account you want to reconcile. Choose the Activities⇨Reconcile command or click Recon on the iconbar.

If you're reconciling a bank account, Quicken displays a dialog box that asks for the beginning and ending bank statement balances, any service charges, and any interest income. (I tell you how to reconcile a credit-card account a little later.) Fill in this information and choose OK.

Quicken next displays another dialog box that lists all your register transactions. You mark the payments and deposits that have cleared the bank by clicking in the Clr column. When you click there, Quicken puts a check mark in the Clr column. It also adjusts the Cleared Balance and the Difference (in the lower right corner of the dialog box).

You know you're done when the difference between the bank statement ending balance and your cleared balance equals zero. Now you can click Finished. You get a Reconciliation Complete dialog box. As part of this screen, Quicken asks if you want to print a reconciliation report. Click Yes or No.

Did you notice that the Clr column in the register now has a bunch of Rs in it? That's to show that your transactions have cleared the bank and been reconciled.

Part IV of this book has some very good advice about what to do if you can't reconcile a bank account.

Steps

❶

❷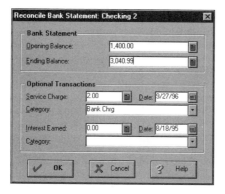

❸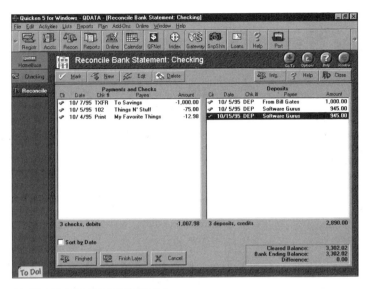

❹

More Stuff

When you pay a credit-card bill, simply record a check in the usual way and categorize the credit-card spending. But, if you've set up a credit-card account, you can transfer the money to the credit-card account as you write the check to pay off (or pay part of) the credit-card bill.

How you handle credit-card payments is up to you. But, if you want to reconcile your credit-card charges and pay all or part of your credit-card charges at the same time, you can (and should) use the Activities⇨Reconcile command.

Display the Register window for the credit-card account you want to reconcile and choose the Activities⇨Reconcile Card Bill command or click Recon on the iconbar.

Quicken displays a dialog box that asks for the charges you've made, the payments you made, the new credit-card balance, and any finance charges you've incurred. (All of this information comes right off your credit-card statement.) Enter the information Quicken wants, and then choose OK.

Quicken displays the Pay Credit Card Bill window, which lists both the charges and the payments. You simply indicate which charges and payments have been received by the credit-card company by clicking them. Click. Click-click. Click. Quicken places a check mark next to each clicked transaction to show you've marked it as cleared. When you've clicked all the cleared transactions, the difference shown in the lower right corner should equal zero.

When the difference does equal zero, choose Finished.

If the difference doesn't equal zero, but you've had enough anyway, choose Finished. In this case, Quicken asks whether you just want to postpone the reconciliation — usually the best idea — or if you want to force your records to agree with the credit card.

If you choose Finished and the credit-card account balances — or you choose Finished even though it doesn't balance, but you tell Quicken that you want to adjust the account — Quicken asks whether you want to make a payment on the credit card. Quicken asks this burning question with a dialog box.

To answer the question, you just fill out the dialog box. Specify on which bank account the check should be written. After you've done this, choose OK. Quicken then displays the appropriate window — Write Checks or the Register — and you describe the check in the usual way.

Steps

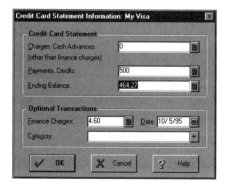

❷

❸

Activities⇨Update Balances⇨
Update Cash Balance

You use this command when you've set up an investment account that includes a cash balance that has somehow gotten goofed up, and you want to fix the cash balance so that it agrees with your brokerage statement.

How You Use It

Display the investment account with the goofed-up cash balance. Choose the Acti̲vities⇨U̲pdate Balances⇨Update C̲ash Balance command. When Quicken displays the Update Cash Balance dialog box, enter the correct cash balance, the date the balance is correct, and the adjustment category.

Steps

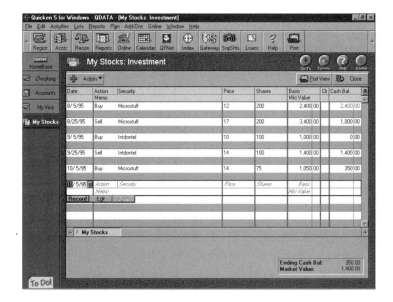

More Stuff

Investment accounts come in two types: mutual fund investment accounts and brokerage investment accounts. Only brokerage investment accounts have a cash account. Mutual fund accounts don't have cash because you own shares in mutual fund accounts. Quicken therefore disables this command if the displayed investment account is a mutual fund account.

Activities⇨Update Balances⇨ Update Share Balance

You use this command when you've got an investment account that has a goofed-up share balance. It does happen, sometimes.

How You Use It

Display the investment account with the goofed-up share balance. Choose the Activities⇨Update Balances⇨Update Share Balance command. When Quicken displays the Update Share Balance dialog box, enter the correct share balance and the date the balance is correct.

A brokerage investment account can have more than one type of security in it. So, if you're adjusting the share balance of a brokerage account, Quicken also asks that you name the security. Answering this question eliminates any confusion, and it makes Quicken's job easier.

Steps

❶

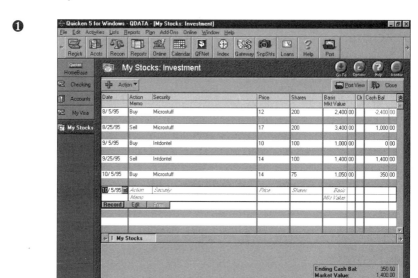

❷

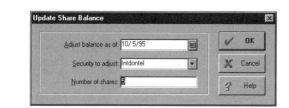

More Stuff

Here's a bit of a quirk. You can actually have more than one
security in a mutual fund investment account. Quicken lets you
do this. You can't, however, specify the security for which you're
updating an incorrect share balance in a mutual fund account.
Quicken just doesn't let you do this. Because of this mysterious
contradiction and the ever-so-slim chance that you may some day
goof up your mutual fund share balance, you should use one
mutual fund account for each mutual fund you own.

Here are a couple of general rules regarding investment accounts: First, you should usually set up one investment account for each statement you receive. Second, if the statement shows only one security and shows no cash, then you can use a mutual fund investment. Otherwise, you'll need to use a brokerage account.

Activities⇨Financial Calendar

While you'll usually want to view your account information in a register, you can also view it in a calendar. With this view, checks and deposits appear as names and amounts on different calendar days, and account balances appear in a bar chart.

How You Use It

To see and use this calendar view of your finances, display the account you want to view in a Register window. Then choose the Activities⇨Financial Calendar command.

Click Prev or Next on the left and right of the month name to move backward and forward a month at a time.

You can use the Options button to customize the Financial Calendar in all sorts of interesting ways (in case you've forgotten, the Options button is the one with a square, a circle, and a triangle on it). When you click the Options button, Quicken shows you the Calendar Options dialog box.

For example, you can select the account (or accounts) you want to view from the Accounts tab of the Calendar Options dialog box. From the QuickFill tab, you can mess with a whole bunch of settings, including whether transactions are memorized automatically and whether fields are completed automatically.

If you really want to have some fun, go back to the Financial Calendar window and find the second button from the left, the one that says View and shows a pair of horn-rimmed glasses. Click it and click the Show Account Graph option. A bar graph appears along the bottom of the window that plots your financial condition.

 If you'd like to write a note to yourself on the calendar, click the date where you want the note to be and then click the leftmost button. When you click Note, Quicken displays a dialog box. The box looks suspiciously like a Post-It™ note. It's even yellow. You fill this box with your note, thought, or comment: **Remember anniversary. Pick up milk. Pay loan shark.**

To close the Financial Calendar window, snap your fingers and click the Close button, the one on the far right.

Steps

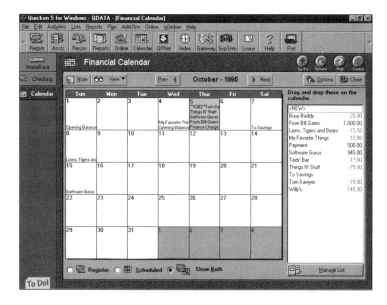

❶

❷

❸

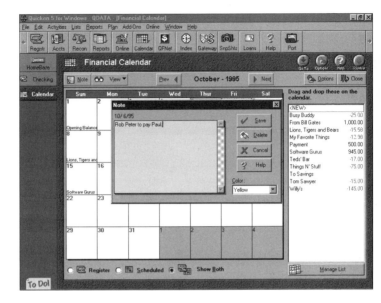

More Stuff

You can enter memorized transactions into the register by selecting them from the list box on the right half of the calendar and then dragging them to the correct day. Quicken considers transactions you enter this way to be *scheduled transactions.* Quicken reminds you of scheduled transactions three days in advance — it figures if all you've done is a bit of clicking and dragging, there's probably a check you still need to handwrite or print. (To learn about scheduled transactions, read the Lists⇨Scheduled Transaction entry in this book.)

The option buttons along the bottom of the Financial Calendar window let you control what sorts of transactions Quicken sticks on the calendar — just regular ol' register transactions, scheduled transactions you've created by dragging memorized transactions to the calendar (as described in the preceding paragraph), or both.

Click the Manage List button below the list of transactions to display the Memorized Transaction List window. From this window, you can create, edit, and delete memorized transactions.

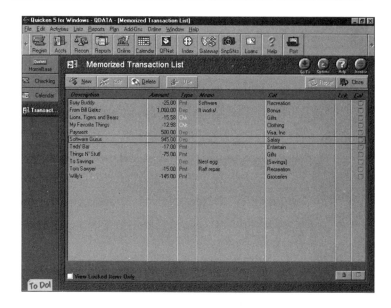

Can't find the <u>M</u>anage List button? That's probably because the bar graph along the bottom of the screen is covering it up. Pull down the V<u>i</u>ew menu and select the Show <u>A</u>ccount Graph option again. It's a toggle command; once you click it, the graph disappears.

Activities ⇨ *Loans*

You aren't limited to tracking bank accounts and credit cards in Quicken. You can also track other things, such as loans. Your mortgage. The car lease. That student loan you took out your last quarter in college even though you really shouldn't have.

To track loans, you need to set up a special type of account, called a *liability account,* and you need to describe how you'll repay the loan. This process is a bit tricky, so Quicken provides a helping hand in the form of this command.

How You Use It

To set up a loan, first collect the paperwork that describes the loan, the payments you're making, and the current loan balance. Then choose the Activities⇨L<u>o</u>ans command. Quicken displays the View Loans dialog box.

Choose the New command button to alert Quicken that you're a little bit scared but still willing to go to the work of setting up your account. Quicken displays the Loan Setup dialog box.

The Loan Setup dialog box asks you for a bunch of information about the loan. Don't panic. Just take it a step at a time. You're asked for the length (or amortization term), when the final payment is due, whether there's a balloon payment (a big lump-sum payment made toward the end of a mortgage) due before the end of the amortization term, the original loan balance, the number of payments a year, the current balance, and the date you originally borrowed the money.

Okay. It's a lot of information. But it's all information that you should know anyway. And, if you've got the original loan paper-work, you'll find this dialog box pretty easy to fill out. Use the mouse or the Tab key to move between the boxes and buttons. Use the keyboard to fill in any of the boxes. When you're done, choose OK.

Quicken now displays a Set Up Loan Payment dialog box. It asks about the loan payments: the interest rate, any additional amounts you include with the interest and principal payments, the payee name, address, and memo description that should go on the check, the next payment date, the category, and whether the transaction should be a memorized transaction, a scheduled transaction, or a checkfree transaction.

You enter this information either by filling in boxes or by clicking command buttons to display other dialog boxes into which you enter information. Sure, there are a lot of boxes to fill. Even so, as long as you have the original loan paperwork, filling in the boxes doesn't take long and is relatively easy. When you're done, choose OK.

Quicken returns you to the View Loans dialog box. It now describes the loan you just set up. Click the Payment Schedule tab to see a schedule of the principal and interest payments you're supposed to make over the life of the loan. (This schedule is called an *amortization schedule* because it shows how loan payments break down into interest and principal.)

Click the Payment Graph tab to see one of those picture-is-worth-a-thousand-words images of how you're going to pay off the loan over time.

Steps

❸

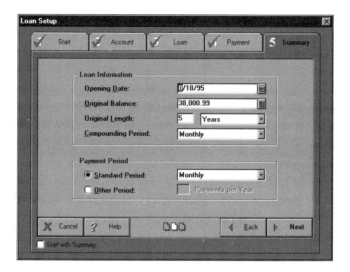

❹

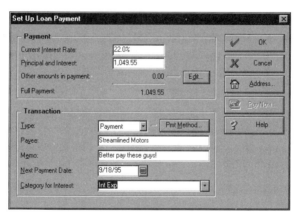

❺

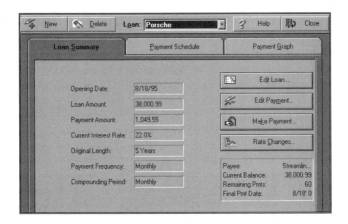

❻

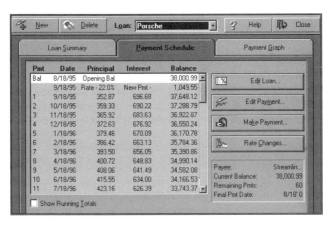

❼

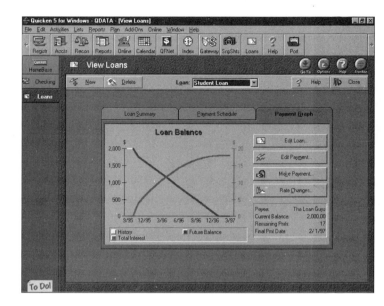

More Stuff

When you make the next loan payment, just enter the payment in the usual way. When you type the payee name, Quicken knows the payee is a lender. So, if you let Quicken fill in the transaction boxes — payee, amount, memo, category, and so on — it uses the loan information. The neat part about all this is that Quicken uses the amortization-schedule information from the View Loans dialog box to fill in the split-transaction information. The principal portion of the loan payment is transferred from your checking account to the loan account, reducing both accounts' balances. The interest portion of the loan payment is categorized as some expense category.

Oh, I should mention one other thing, too. The View Loans dialog box, which gets displayed when you choose the Activities⇨Loans command, provides three command buttons for updating loan information: Edit Loan, Edit Payment, and Rate Changes. To use these command buttons to update the information on a loan, first activate the Edit Loan drop-down list box to identify the loan (you can find this drop-down list at the very top of the window, in the center). After you've chosen a loan:

- Use the Edit Loan command button to display the Edit Loan dialog box and change some of the information you entered when you described the loan balance and term the first time around.

- Use the Edit Payment command button to display the Set Up Loan Payment dialog box and change some of the information you entered there to describe the payment transaction.

- When you've borrowed money using an adjustable interest rate loan, use the Rate Changes command button to display a dialog box that lets you enter the new interest rates and the dates those rates become effective.

And guess what? You can even record a loan payment straight from the View Loans dialog box. Click the Make Payment command button and Quicken asks you, via another dialog box, whether the payment is a regularly scheduled payment or not. Click Regular or Extra, and then tell Quicken to whom to make out the check. Click OK and you hear that beeping sound. You should recognize that sound. It means that Quicken has recorded the check payment in your register.

Activities⇨Portfolio View

If you set up investment accounts, you aren't limited to viewing investment transactions and account information in the Register window. You can also view investment transactions and account balances in the Portfolio View window.

How You Use It

If you've set up at least one investment account, simply choose the Activities⇨Portfolio View command or click the Port icon on the iconbar. Quicken displays the Portfolio View window.

By clicking the Action button at the top of the Portfolio View window, you can get a drop-down menu for recording investment transactions: additional share purchases, a fat dividend, some almost unconscionable capital gain.

You can also click the Report command button to produce a quick-and-dirty report about the selected security. If you're plugged into Quicken by modem, and you've attached ticker symbols to your securities, you can get the latest prices on your securities by clicking the Update button.

Click the Options command button and then the Miscellaneous and Custom View tabs to change what the Portfolio window displays. For example, you can specify the date as of which you want to see investment information, the investment account, and the type of information you want to view.

I could spend a lot of time talking about all these options. In fact, my own *Quicken 5 For Windows For Dummies* book spends two or three chapters on this material. I don't have room for that here, however. So let me throw out this suggestion: experiment with the Portfolio Options View dialog box. You can't get into any trouble. You won't change the investment account information — only the way it's displayed.

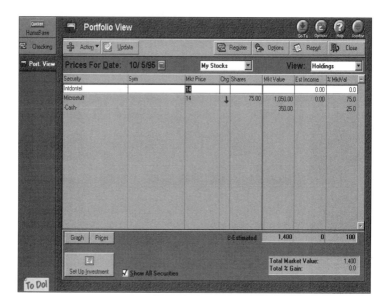

More Stuff

Along the bottom edge of the Portfolio View window are the Set Up New Investment, Prices, and Graph command buttons. Click Set Up New Investment to start recording another investment account. Click Graph to get a nice, in-your-face look at how your investments are doing. Click Prices to get the price history for your investment account.

Activities⇨Recategorize

You can use the Activities⇨Recategorize command to change a category for all the transactions in an account. Suppose — just for the sake of illustration — that you've been assigning all your recreational expenses to Entertainment but now want to recategorize at least some of those transactions as Education. What do you do? Well, you can use the Activities⇨ Recategorize command.

How You Use It

Open the register. When you choose the Activities⇨Recategorize command, Quicken displays the Recategorize dialog box.

Describe the transactions you're looking for by using the Search Category box. For this the sample search, you enter **Entertainment.** You can enter category names by typing them yourself or by using the pull-down list. When you're done, select Find All. Quicken displays a list of the transactions that include the category you selected — Entertainment.

Next, use the Replace With box to describe the replacement category that you want to use and mark the transactions that you want to change. In this case, you would enter **Education** by typing it or selecting it from the pull-down list. To mark a transaction, just click in the empty column to its left. Or click the Mark All button at the bottom of the dialog box if you want to mark all the transactions.

When you select the Replace button, Quicken displays a message box asking you to confirm your replacements. Assuming you click Yes, it displays another message box telling you about the replacements it has made.

Steps

①

②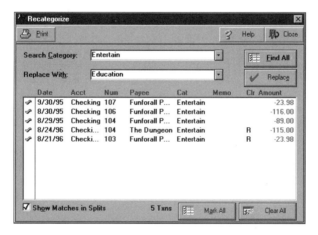

③

More Stuff

See those two buttons at the bottom of the Recategorize window? Click Mark All when you want to change the categories of all the transactions you've found. Click Clear All if you've marked several transactions but have changed your mind. Clear All takes all the check marks out of the left-hand column.

Activities⇨Use Calculator

The Activities⇨Use Calculator command displays a pop-up calculator that you can use to make quick calculations. You can also paste the number shown on the calculator display right into a field.

How You Use It

Just choose this command. When Quicken displays the calculator, click the calculator's number keys and operator keys. For example, to calculate two plus two, click 2, +, 2, and then = (the equal key). Ah, yes. 4.

Steps

❶

➋

More Stuff

I'll give you a quick rundown on the other calculator keys, too. To clear the display, click C (the clear key). To clear the last number or operator entered, click CE (the clear entry key). To remove the last digit typed, click <- (the clear digit key).

The MS, MR, and MC keys work with the calculator's memory. MS stores the number on the calculator display in the memory. MR recalls the number stored in the memory. MC clears the memory.

Let me mention one other interesting tidbit. After you open the calculator, Quicken leaves it on top of any other windows. So it always lies over the top of some portion of the Quicken desktop or application window. If, for some reason, you don't want Quicken to do this, you need to activate the calculator's Control menu and uncheck the Always On Top command. (You can activate the calculator's Control menu by clicking its Control menu box — the little calculator icon in the upper left corner of the calculator.)

Activities⇨Reminders

The Activities⇨Reminders command displays the Quicken Reminders window. Why might you do this? To see whether you've got any unprinted checks that should probably be printed, any scheduled transactions that should probably be entered into some register, and any calendar notes (from the Financial Calendar) that should probably be read.

This command can be used with the Activities⇨Financial Calendar command.

How You Use It

Choose this command. Use the Show Notes for drop-down list to specify for which week you want to see calendar notes. Click the Checks to Print button (if it's not grayed out) to start the whole check-printing thing. Click the Scheduled Transactions Due button (if it's not grayed out) to enter any scheduled transactions that need to be entered. If you don't have checks to print or scheduled transactions, you won't be able to choose the Checks to Print or Scheduled Transactions Due button, of course.

If you're one of those lucky souls who is plugged into Quicken's online features, the Online Bill Payment and Online Banking buttons will be activated. You can click them to schedule an electronic payment or electronic bank transaction.

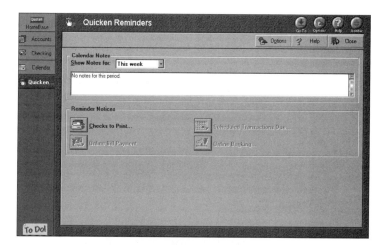

Activities⇨Order Checks

Quicken wants your business — if you doubt me, just choose this command. It gives you the golden opportunity to purchase everything from Quicken except the kitchen sink.

How You Use It

Choose Activities⇨Order Checks, and you see a wide-angle screen that says "Intuit Marketplace." Press any key to get to the computer-screen equivalent of a department store. From here, you can buy all sorts of things, some of which are even useful.

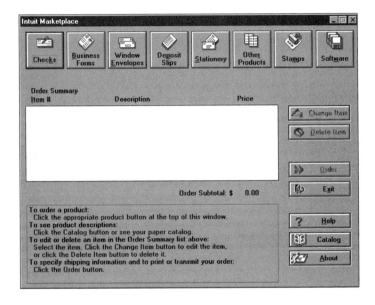

More Stuff

I'm not sure what the ethics of selling goods by way of computer software programs are. In any case, you can figure out how to use the Intuit Marketplace window on your own.

Lists Menu Commands

The Lists menu commands display windows that list and let you change accounts, categories, classes, memorized transactions, scheduled transactions, securities, security types, investment goals, and memorized investment transactions. All the commands work the same way — in terms of their mechanics. The only difference is that they display different lists.

Lists⇨Account

The Lists⇨Account command opens the Account List window.
You can use this window to get a quick list of account balances.
You can also use it to create new accounts, delete existing
accounts, and edit some of the account information.

How You Use It

Choose the Lists⇨Account command (you can also click Accts
on the iconbar). When you do this, Quicken displays the Account
List window, which lists all the accounts you've created.

To close the Account List window, click the Close button, the
rightmost button in the row of buttons.

To activate another window without closing the Account List
window, click a QuickTab on the left side of the screen or use one
of the Window menu commands. If you can see the other window
you want to activate, click it.

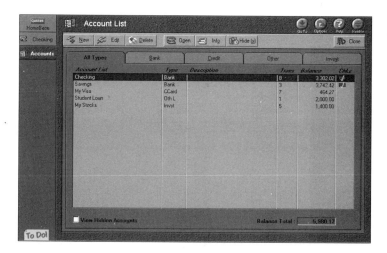

More Stuff

If you've chosen the Lists⇨Account command, and the Account
List window shows on your screen, you may be wondering about
those command buttons across the top of the window. If so, here
are some quick descriptions:

- The <u>N</u>ew button starts the Create New Account dialog box so you can create a new account. (If you choose this button, the first dialog box you see asks you to select an account type.)

- The Ed<u>i</u>t button displays a dialog box that lets you change the account name and description.

- The <u>D</u>elete button removes the selected account and all its transactions.

- The O<u>p</u>en button displays the selected account's register. You can also display a register by double-clicking the account in the account list.

- The Inf<u>o</u> button displays a dialog box you can use to collect and store additional information about an account.

- The Hide button lets you keep an account from being seen on the account list. Select an account, click the Hide button, and take the check mark out of the View Hidden Acco<u>u</u>nts check box at the bottom of the window. The account disappears. Click the Hide button once more if you need to see the account again.

- The Close button closes, or removes, the Account List window.

You can use the tabs that appear at the top of the account list box — All T<u>y</u>pes, <u>B</u>ank, <u>C</u>redit, O<u>t</u>her, and Inve<u>s</u>t — to specify which accounts the Account List box lists.

Lists⇨Category & Transfer

The <u>L</u>ists⇨<u>C</u>ategory & Transfer command opens the Category & Transfer List window. In a nutshell, this window shows the category and account names you can plug into the category boxes of the Register and Write Checks windows.

How You Use It

Choose the <u>L</u>ists⇨<u>C</u>ategory & Transfer command. When you do, Quicken displays the Category & Transfer List window, which lists all the categories you can use and all the accounts you've created. (You use account names in the category box when you record transfers between accounts.)

If you want to select a category or account name from the list and copy it to the category box you were just trying to fill in a Register or Write Checks window, double-click the category or account name.

To close the Category & Transfer List window when you're done fooling with it, click the Close button.

To activate another window without closing the Category & Transfer List window, click a QuickTab on the left side of the screen or use one of the Window menu commands. Or, if you can see the other window you want to activate, just click it with the mouse.

More Stuff

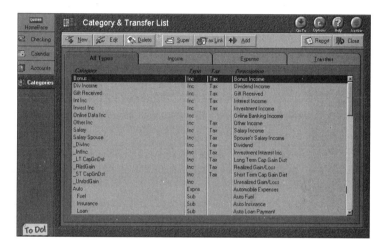

What do those mysterious buttons along the top of the screen do? Good question.

- Click New, the one with the red cross on it, to display a dialog box you can use to add a new category or subcategory.

- Click Edit, the one with a pencil and a red tapeworm, to see the Edit Category dialog box, where you can change the category name, description, and type.

- Next is the Delete button, which you can press when you want to remove the selected category.

- Super, which shows a folder spilling open, is for creating and managing supercategories.

- Tax Link, the button with a money bag and a sheet of paper, is for assigning expense and income categories to lines on standard tax forms.

- The Add button displays the Add Categories dialog box when you click it. From this dialog box, you can add categories from Quicken's Home or Business Category list to your own list of expense and income categories.

- Use the Report button, which is over next to the Close button, to print a report of transactions using the selected category.

Lists⇨*Class*

The Lists⇨Class command opens the Class List window. This window shows the class names you can plug into the category boxes (following the category names) of the Register and Write Checks windows. Classes give you a second way to summarize the transactions in a register.

This second-way-to-summarize business may sound confusing, but think of it this way. Say you're a real-estate investor. You might use categories to summarize types of rental income, such as rent, laundry room charges, and late fees, and to summarize types of expenses, such as insurance, maintenance, and utilities. You might use classes to summarize income and expenses by individual properties: the rental house on Baltic Avenue, the hotel on Boardwalk, and so on.

How You Use It

Choose the Lists⇨Class command. When you do, Quicken displays the Class List window, which lists all the classes.

If you're in the Write Checks window or a register, and you want to record a class for the transaction you're recording, select Lists⇨Class, choose a class from the list, and double-click it. The class name appears in the transaction recording after a slash. If you've recorded a category as well as a class, you see something like this: Rental income/Park Place.

To close the Class List window, click the Close button.

To activate another window without closing the Class List window, click a QuickTab on the left side of the screen, use one of the Window menu commands, or just click the window if you can see it.

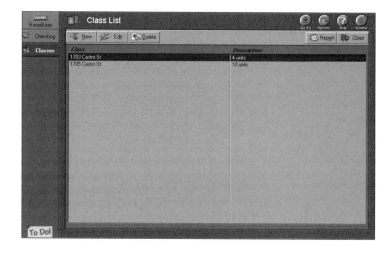

More Stuff

- The <u>N</u>ew button displays a dialog box you can use to add a new class or subclass.

- The Ed<u>i</u>t button displays a dialog box that lets you change the class name and description.

- The <u>D</u>elete button removes the selected class. Be careful with this one. As soon as you click it, you hear the beep-beep sound, and your class is gone in a puff of smoke, a bit like the one Wile E. Coyote made when he hit the bottom of the canyon. You can't get your class back.

- The Rep<u>o</u>rt button generates a report of transactions classified with the selected class.

<u>Lists</u>⇨Memorized <u>T</u>ransaction

The <u>L</u>ists⇨Memorized <u>T</u>ransaction command opens the Memorized Transaction List window. This window shows the memorized transactions you can use and reuse.

You actually don't need to use the Memorized Transactions command or its list, however. As neat as memorized transactions sound, they're redundant. Quicken's QuickFill feature lets you reuse transactions without having to worry about memorizing and without having to display a list of memorized transactions. Why? Because QuickFill automatically memorizes transactions, and it automatically reuses, or recalls, them.

How You Use It

Choose the Lists⇨Memorized Transaction command. When you do, Quicken displays the Memorized Transaction List window, which lists all the memorized transactions.

To choose a memorized transaction from the list and copy it to the selected register row or the Write Checks window, double-click it.

To close the Memorized Transaction List window, click the Close button.

To activate another window without closing the Memorized Transaction List window, use its numbered Window menu command, click a QuickTab on the left side of the screen, or just click the window if you can see it.

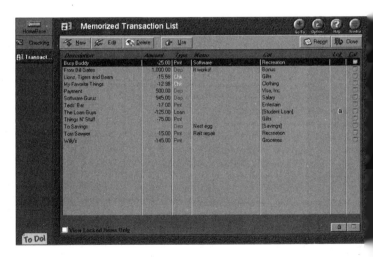

More Stuff

- Clicking the New button displays a dialog box you can use to add a new memorized transaction to the list, but this is the hard way to create new memorized transactions. By far, it's easiest to select a transaction in the Register window and choose the Edit⇨Memorize Transaction command.

- The Edit button displays a dialog box that lets you change the memorized transaction.

- The Delete button removes the selected memorized transaction.

- Click the Use button to record the memorized transaction in the Write Checks window or the register.

- The Report button prints a report of transactions created with the selected memorized transaction. This is a quick way to see how much you've spent on, or earned from, transactions.

You can have Quicken remove memorized transactions from the transaction list after a period of months has elapsed. If you haven't written a check to somebody in, say, the last two months, you can have Quicken take that somebody off the transaction list automatically. Here's how: select Edit⇨Options, click the General button, put a check in the Remove Memorized Transactions Not Used in Last Months check box, and enter a **2** in the little box to the right that says "months." By pruning the transaction list this way, you don't have to search as far through the list when you want to select a memorized transaction, because the list is shorter.

Lists⇨Scheduled Transaction

The Lists⇨Scheduled Transaction command opens the Scheduled Transaction List window. This window shows the scheduled transactions that Quicken either reminds you to enter or automatically enters for you on a specified schedule. These transactions might include a mortgage payment that the lender automatically withdraws on the 10th of each month, or your semi-monthly payroll check that's automatically deposited by your employer.

How You Use It

Choose the Lists⇨Scheduled Transaction command. When you do, Quicken displays the Scheduled Transaction List window, which lists any transactions you have scheduled.

To make a scheduled transaction on the list, select it and click the Pay command button. Quicken enters and records the transaction in the correct account register.

To close the Scheduled Transaction List window, click the Close button.

To activate another window without closing the Scheduled Transaction List window, use its numbered Window menu command, click the other window, or click a QuickTab on the left side of the screen.

Steps

❶

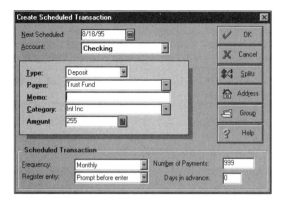

More Stuff

Click the New button to see a dialog box you can use to add a new scheduled transaction. When Quicken displays the dialog box, you just fill in the blanks.

Edit displays a dialog box that lets you change the transaction that is selected in the Scheduled Transaction list. For example, you can change the date, the amount, the payee name, or anything else, for that matter.

Delete removes the selected scheduled transaction. Be careful of this one. As soon as you click Delete, the transaction is gone.

Lists⇨Security

The Lists⇨Security command opens the Security List window. This window lists the securities — stocks, bonds, and mutual fund shares — for which you can record investment transactions. This command isn't difficult to use, but I'll warn you that investment record-keeping can get rather involved if you've gotten tricky in your investing.

How You Use It

Choose the Lists⇨Security command. When you do, Quicken displays the Security List window, which lists all the securities you've set up. From here you can track security investments, edit or delete investments, get reports on investments, and even start a new security investment account.

To add a new security to the list, select the <u>N</u>ew command button. When Quicken displays a dialog box, fill in its blanks.

To close the Security List window, click the Close button.

To activate another window without closing the Security List window, use its numbered <u>W</u>indow menu command, click the other window if you can see it, or click a QuickTab on the left side of the screen.

Steps

❶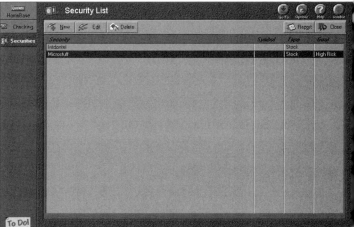

❷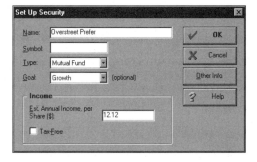

More Stuff

The Ed_i_t button displays a dialog box that lets you change the selected security's name, symbol, type, goal, tax-deferred status, and estimated annual income.

The _D_elete button removes the selected security.

The Rep_o_rt button produces a report listing all the transactions for the selected security.

Lists⇨_Security Type_

The _L_ists⇨Security T_y_pe command opens the Security Type List window. This window lists categories you can use to summarize your securities. By default, it lists five security types: Bond, CD, Futures, Mutual Fund, and Stock.

How You Use It

When you choose the _L_ists⇨Security T_y_pe command, Quicken displays the Security Type List window, which lists the security types Quicken provides and any security types you've set up.

To add a new security type to the list, you select the _N_ew command button. When Quicken displays the Set Up Security Type dialog box, fill in the text box. You also need to use the Price Display radio buttons — Decimal and Fraction — to indicate how Quicken should display prices for securities of this type.

To close the Security List window, click the Close button.

To activate another window without closing the Security List window, use its numbered _W_indow menu command, click the other window if you can see it, or click a QuickTab on the left side of the screen.

Steps

❶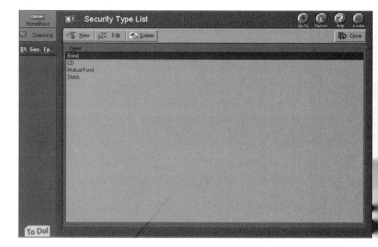

❷

More Stuff

To change a security type name or price display, choose the security on the Security Type List and select Ed̲it. Quicken displays a dialog box that lets you make your changes.

The D̲elete button removes the selected security type from the list in case you don't want to see it there. By the way, you can't delete a security type from the list if you've recorded securities of that type. Nope, Quicken won't let you do that.

Lists⇨Investment Goal

The Lists⇨Investment Goal command opens the Investment Goal List window. This window lists goals you can use to summarize your securities. By default, it lists five investment goals: College Fund, Growth, High Risk, Income, and Low Risk. Once you've set up an investment goal with this command, you can use the goal as a way to see whether your investments are helping to achieve your goal.

It may just be me, but creating a goal-based summarization system for individual securities seems borderline kooky. So do some of the default investment goals. (Who, for example, specifies High Risk as a formal investment goal?)

How You Use It

Choose the Lists⇨Investment Goal command. When you do, Quicken displays the Investment Goal List window, which lists the investment goals Quicken provides as well as any investment goals you've set up.

To add a new investment goal to the list, select the New command button. When Quicken displays a dialog box, fill in its blank. (That's right — it's "blank," not "blanks.") You might enter "Early Retirement," "Buy the Farm," or "Get that Porsche."

To close the Investment Goal List window, click the Close button.

Once you've added a goal to the list, you can attach it to a security account. Choose Lists⇨Security, select the account, click the Edit button in the Security List window, choose a goal from the Goal drop-down list, and click OK. Now, when you choose Choose Lists⇨Security, you see the new goal in the Goal column. Click the security and examine it to see whether you're getting near your goal.

To activate another window without closing the Investment Goal List window, use its numbered Window menu command, click the other window, or select a QuickTab on the left side of the screen.

Steps

❶

❷

More Stuff

To change an investment goal, select it on the list and choose Edit. Quicken displays a dialog box that lets you make your change.

To remove an investment goal, select it and choose Delete. Now the goal doesn't appear in the Goal column of the Security List window.

Lists⇨Memorized Investment Trans

The Lists⇨Memorized Investment Trans command opens the Investment Transaction List window. This command is a fast way to enter a memorized investment transaction in a register row or the Write Checks window.

How You Use It

From the Write Checks window or the last row in an investment register, choose the Lists⇨Memorized Investment Trans command. When you do, Quicken displays the Investment Transaction List window, which lists all the memorized investment transactions you can use and reuse.

To choose a memorized investment transaction from the list and copy it to the selected register row or to the Write Checks window, double-click it. If you want to, you can also replace an existing transaction in a register with this command. Select the transaction, choose Lists⇨Memorized Investment Trans, and double-click the transaction in the Investment Transaction List window.

Delete removes the selected memorized investment transaction. Select the transaction before choosing Delete.

To close the Investment Transaction List window, click the Close button.

To activate another window without closing the Investment Transaction List window, use its numbered Window menu command, click the other window if you can see it, or click a QuickTab on the left side of the screen.

More Stuff

To have Quicken memorize an investment transaction, you display an investment Register window (by clicking the Accts icon and double-clicking the account name in the Account List window), select the transaction you want it to memorize, and then choose the Edit⊅Memorize Transaction command.

Reports Menu Commands

The Reports menu commands let you easily produce Quicken's predesigned reports. They also let you create custom reports from scratch and produce a handful of attractive graphs.

Let me say a couple of other things before you start reading any of the command entries that follow. First, it's easy to print reports. You can probably print most of the reports you want with four or five mouse clicks. Second, every Home, Investment, Business, and Other report submenu command displays the very same Create Report dialog box. So to save a few trees by conserving a bit of paper, I'm not going to show you the same Create Report dialog box 60 times. No way, man.

You can also produce reports by clicking the Reports button on the iconbar. When you do, Quicken displays the same Create Report dialog box referenced in the command descriptions that follow.

 One more thing. You can see the last four reports you've created by opening the Reports menu and clicking one of the four reports (numbered 1 through 4) at the bottom of the menu.

Reports⊅EasyAnswers

Choose the Reports⊅EasyAnswers command to get a quick-and-dirty report about some aspect of your finances. You can find out how much you spent altogether, how much you spent on one of your categories, how much you saved in different time periods, your net worth, and whether you made budget or not.

How You Use It

Choose Reports⇨EasyAnswers, and Quicken shows you the EasyAnswers tab of the Create Report dialog box. On this tab are five questions about your financial records.

Pick the question you want the answer to and, using the drop-down menus, choose the particulars. For example, you can find out where you spent your money last year, this month, this year, this quarter, this month to date, this year to date, and so on. After you fill in the particulars, either click the button to the left of the question or click the Create button at the bottom of the dialog box.

Quicken shows you an exhaustive report that answers your all-important question. Actually, how exhaustive the report is depends on how much data you entered. If you've only recorded transactions for this year, for example, you can't get a report on your spending for last year.

Likewise, if you haven't done any budgeting, Quicken refuses to give you a budgeting report (the last report on the EasyAnswers tab).

 Once the report is on-screen, you can check out the details. Move the cursor over the part of the report you'd like to know more about. If the cursor turns into a magnifying glass, you can click the mouse to learn more. Quicken either shows you a QuickZoom Report that scrutinizes your finances even closer, or it shows you the transaction in the register that you "zoomed on."

Steps

❶

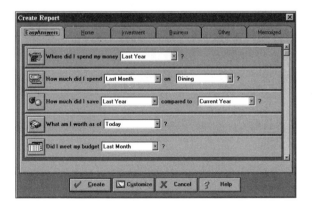

❷

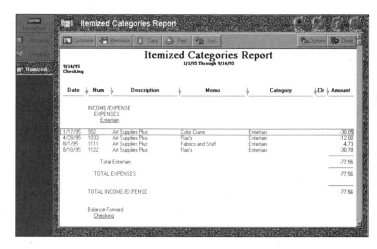

More Stuff

Notice those buttons along the top of the Itemized Categories
Report window?

- With the Customize button, you can change the dates, the
  categories, and the way the table is laid out.

- Click the Memorize button (the one that looks like a floppy
  disk) if you've worked up a customized report of your own
  and you want to be able to generate reports such as your
  new report again. When you click this button, a dialog box
  appears so you can give the report a name and call upon it
  later on.

- Click the Copy button to, you guessed it, copy the report to
  the Clipboard.

- You can print the on-screen version of the report by
  selecting the Print button. Quicken displays the Print
  Report dialog box. Use its Print to option buttons and other
  options to indicate how Quicken should print the report.
  Then select OK.

- The Sort button is for sorting, or rearranging, the information on the report and getting a different presentation.
  When you click this button, a dialog box appears so you
  can give Quicken a category — Payee name or date, for
  example — to sort the data on.

- The Options button, the second one from the right, gives you more ways of generating the report. You can choose a new date range or different categories, for example.

- To close the report's document window, select the command button farthest to the right.

Reports⇨Home⇨Cash Flow

The Reports⇨Home⇨Cash Flow command opens the Create Report dialog box to the Home tab. This command also fills in the Report Dates boxes to produce a report of your year-to-date income and expenses summarized by category.

How You Use It

Choose the Reports⇨Home⇨Cash Flow command. When you do, Quicken displays the Home tab of the Create Report dialog box and highlights the Cash Flow reports selection. Use the Report Dates drop-down list box and the from and to boxes to specify the time interval you want to summarize. Then choose the Cash Flow button or click Create. Quicken displays an on-screen version of the report.

Steps

❶

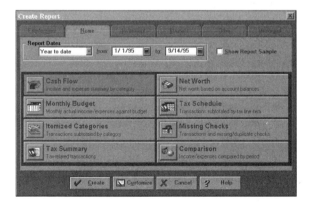

❷

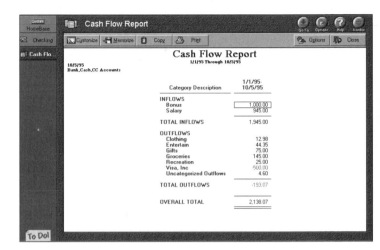

More Stuff

To print the on-screen version of the report, select the Print command button. Quicken displays the Print Report dialog box. Use its Print to and other radio buttons to indicate how Quicken should print the report. Then select OK.

To close the report's document window, select the Close command button.

You can customize the cash-flow report in all sorts of ways by selecting the Customize command button on the Create Report dialog box or the Customize command button at the top of the Cash Flow Report window. Either way, Quicken displays a dialog box you can use to describe how you want the report to appear.

You can have Quicken memorize a cash-flow report by selecting the Memorize command button, which appears at the top of the Cash Flow Report window.

You can copy a report to the Windows Clipboard by selecting the Copy command button. You might choose this command button to move a report to a spreadsheet program, such as Microsoft Excel.

Reports⇨Home⇨Monthly Budget

The Reports⇨Home⇨Monthly Budget command opens the
Create Report dialog box. This command also fills in the Report
Dates drop-down lists to produce a report comparing your year-
to-date income and expenses (summarized by category) with
your budget.

How You Use It

To produce a monthly budget report, you first need to set up a
budget by using the Plan⇨Budgeting command. Once you've
completed this prerequisite, choose the Reports⇨Home⇨Monthly
Budget command.

When you follow these steps, Quicken displays the Home tab of
the Create Report dialog box and highlights the Monthly Budget
selection. Use the Report Dates drop-down list box and the from
and to boxes to specify the time interval for which you want to
compare actual and budgeted amounts. Then click either the
Monthly Budget button or click Create. Quicken displays an
on-screen version of the report.

More Stuff

You can customize the Monthly Budget report, memorize it, copy
it to the Windows Clipboard, print it, and close its report window
in the same way you do for a cash-flow report. (See Reports⇨
Home⇨Cash Flow.)

Reports⇨Home⇨Itemized Categories

The Reports⇨Home⇨Itemized Categories command opens the
Create Report dialog box to the Home tab. This command also
fills in the Report Dates to produce a report that lists and
summarizes individual transactions by category. See also the
Reports⇨Home⇨Cash Flow command.

How You Use It

When you choose the Reports⇨Home⇨Itemized Categories command, Quicken displays the Home tab of the Create Report dialog box and highlights the Itemized Categories Report. Use the Report Dates drop-down list box to specify the time interval for which you want to list and summarize individual transactions. Then choose the Itemized Categories button or click Create. Quicken displays an on-screen version of the report.

This report describes spending in all your expense and income categories, which makes for a very long report. Still, you can scroll down the pages and get very useful summaries of where you're dropping money and taking it in.

More Stuff

You can customize the Itemized Categories Report, memorize it, copy it to the Windows Clipboard, print it, and close its report window in the same way you do a cash-flow report. (See Reports⇨Home⇨Cash Flow.)

You can sort transactions that are summarized by category by selecting the Sort button. Click this button to see a dialog box with a drop-down list box that presents the various sort options.

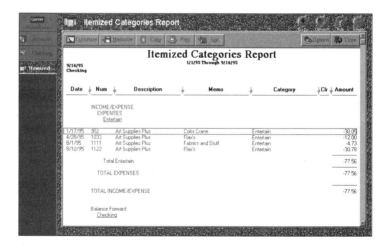

Reports⇨Home⇨Tax Summary

The Reports⇨Home⇨Tax Summary command opens the Create Report dialog box to the Home tab. This command also fills in the Report Dates to produce a report that lists and summarizes tax-related transactions by category. See also the Reports⇨Home⇨ Cash Flow command.

How You Use It

Choose the Reports⇨Home⇨Tax Summary command. When you do, Quicken displays the Home tab of the Create Report dialog box and highlights the Tax Summary selection. Use the Report Dates drop-down list box to specify the time interval for which you want to list and summarize transactions. Then click the Tax Summary button or click Create. Quicken displays an on-screen version of the report.

More Stuff

You can customize the tax summary report, memorize it, copy it to the Windows Clipboard, print it, and close its report window in the same way you do a cash-flow report. (See Reports⇨Home⇨ Cash Flow.)

You can sort transactions that are summarized by category by selecting the Sort button. When you click this button, you see a dialog box with a drop-down list box that presents the various sort options. Select the one you want, click OK, and your report appears miraculously reorganized in the specified order.

Reports⇨Home⇨Net Worth

The Reports⇨Home⇨Net Worth command opens the Create Report dialog box to the Home tab. This command also fills in the Report Balance as box to produce a report that lists account balances as of today's date, whatever that date happens to be.

To produce a true net-worth report, you must have already set up accounts for all your assets and liabilities. You also need to be keeping accurate records for these assets and liabilities. See also the Reports⇨Home⇨Cash Flow command.

How You Use It

When you choose the Reports⇨Home⇨Net Worth command, Quicken displays the Home tab of the Create Report dialog box. Use the Report Balance as box to specify the date for which Quicken reports account balances. When you select the Net Worth button or click Create, Quicken displays an on-screen version of the report.

If you can't see the Net Worth button because report samples appear on the right side of the dialog box, click the Show Report Sample check box to remove the sample reports and expose the Net Worth button.

Once a report is on-screen, you can check out the details. Move the cursor over the part of the report you'd like to know more about. If the cursor turns into a magnifying glass, you can click the mouse button to see a QuickZoom Report that scrutinizes your finances even closer.

More Stuff

You can customize the net-worth report, memorize it, copy it to the Windows Clipboard, print it, and close its report window in the same way you do for a cash-flow report. (See Reports⇨Home⇨ Cash Flow.)

Reports⇨Home⇨Tax Schedule

The Reports⇨Home⇨Tax Schedule command opens the Create Report dialog box to the Home tab. This command also fills in the Report Dates to produce a report that lists and summarizes tax-related transactions by tax form and tax schedule line number.

If you want to use this report — perhaps you want to export its information to a tax-preparation program such as TurboTax — you need to identify the tax form and tax schedule lines that your category totals should go on.

To do this, you first need to choose the Edit⇨Options command, select the General button on the Options window, and mark the Use Tax Schedules with Categories check box. Then you need to specify, for each and every category, the tax form and line number. (Once you've marked the Use Tax Schedules with Categories check box, Quicken adds a drop-down list box to the Set Up Category and Edit Category dialog boxes for this exact purpose.) See also the Reports⇨Home⇨Cash Flow command.

How You Use It

When you choose the Reports⟹Home⟹Tax Schedule command, Quicken displays the Home tab of the Create Report dialog box. Use the Report Dates drop-down list box to specify the time interval for which Quicken should calculate tax-schedule input figures. When you choose the Tax Schedule button or click Create, Quicken displays an on-screen version of the report.

If you can't see the Tax Schedule button because report samples appear on the right side of the dialog box, click the Show Report Sample check box to remove the sample reports and expose the Tax Schedule button.

More Stuff

You can customize the Tax Schedule report, memorize it, copy it to the Windows Clipboard, print it, and close its report window in the same way you do a cash-flow report. (See Reports⟹Home⟹ Cash Flow.)

You can export the tax-schedule information to a tax export file by selecting the Export command button. It displays a dialog box that you use to name the file and specify its disk and directory location. Be sure to leave the List Files of Type box set to `Tax export files (*.txf)`. This exports the file in a format that a tax-preparation program, such as TurboTax, can easily use.

Reports⟹Home⟹Missing Checks

The Reports⟹Home⟹Missing Checks command opens the Create Report dialog box to the Home tab. This command also fills in the Report Dates to produce a report that lists transactions in order of check number and highlights gaps in the check number sequence. See also the Reports⟹Home⟹Cash Flow command.

How You Use It

When you choose the Reports⇨Home⇨Missing Checks command, Quicken displays the Home tab of the Create Report dialog box. Use the Report Dates drop-down list box and the from and to boxes to specify the time interval for which Quicken should list transactions and flag check-numbering gaps. When you choose the Missing Checks button or click Create, Quicken displays an on-screen version of the report.

If you can't see the Missing Checks button because report samples appear on the right side of the dialog box, click the Show Report Sample check box to remove the sample reports and expose the Missing Checks button.

More Stuff

You can customize missing checks, memorize them, copy them to the Windows Clipboard, print them, and close their report windows in the same way you do a cash-flow report. (See Reports⇨Home⇨Cash Flow.)

Reports⇨Home⇨Comparison

The Reports⇨Home⇨Comparison command opens the Create Report dialog box to the Home tab. This command also fills in the Compare Dates to produce a report that compares income and expense category totals for two time intervals — such as last year's totals and this year's totals. See also the Reports⇨Home⇨ Cash Flow command.

How You Use It

When you choose the Reports⇨Home⇨Comparison command, Quicken displays the Home tab of the Create Report dialog box. Fill in all the Compare Dates boxes to specify the time intervals for which the comparison should be made. Then choose the Comparison button or click Create to have Quicken display an on-screen version of the report.

If you can't see the Comparison button because report samples appear on the right side of the dialog box, click the Show Report Sample check box to remove the sample reports and expose the Comparison button.

More Stuff

You can customize the Comparison report, memorize it, copy it to the Windows Clipboard, print it, and close its report window in the same way you do for a cash-flow report. (See Reports⇨Home⇨ Cash Flow.)

Reports⇨Investment⇨Portfolio Value

The Reports⇨Investment⇨Portfolio Value command opens the Create Report dialog box to the Investment tab. This command also fills in the dialog box to produce a report of your investment portfolio's value as of a specified date.

How You Use It

When you choose the Reports⇨Investment⇨Portfolio Value command, Quicken displays the Investment tab of the Create Report dialog box. Use the Report Value as of box to specify the date for which you want an estimate of your investment portfolio's market value. Then choose the Portfolio Value button or click Create. Quicken displays an on-screen version of the report.

More Stuff

To print the on-screen version of the report, select the Print command button. Quicken displays the Print Report dialog box. Use its Print to and other options to indicate how Quicken should print the report. Then choose OK.

To close the report's window, choose the Close button.

You can customize the portfolio-value report in all sorts of ways by selecting the Customize command button on the Create Report dialog box or the Customize button at the top of the Portfolio Value Report window. Either way, Quicken displays a dialog box that you can use to describe how you want the report to appear.

You can have Quicken memorize a portfolio-value report by selecting the Memorize command button, which appears at the top of the Portfolio Value Report window.

You can copy a report to the Windows Clipboard by selecting the Copy command, which appears at the top of the Portfolio Value Report window. You might choose this command to move a report to a spreadsheet program, such as Microsoft Excel.

Reports⇨Investment⇨Investment Performance

The Reports⇨Investment⇨Investment Performance command opens the Create Report dialog box to the Investment tab. This command also fills in the dialog box to produce a report that calculates the internal rate of return delivered by the securities in your investment portfolio for a specified interval of time.

Internal rates of return can be pretty neat. They let you calculate an annualized *yield,* or return, for securities you would otherwise find impossible to evaluate. With an internal rate of return, for example, you can calculate the effective annualized return for a stock you bought three months ago, which paid a $1 per share dividend two months ago, and, just yesterday, skyrocketed to $6 a share.

There's a practical problem with these calculations, however. If you calculate an internal rate of return for a short period of time — such as a week or a month — you annualize small, irrelevant changes in market value. And this can create ridiculous and meaningless annual return measures. If you annualize a $5 per share price change that occurs some month on a $40 per share stock, for example, you get an internal rate of return equal to roughly 9,000 percent. And, while you may be good, you're probably not *that* good. See also the Reports⇨Investment⇨ Portfolio Value command.

How You Use It

When you choose the Reports⇨Investment⇨Investment Performance command, Quicken displays the Investment tab of the Create Report dialog box. Use the Report Dates drop-down list box and the from and to boxes to describe the time interval for which you want internal rates of return calculated. Then choose the Investment Performance button or click Create. Quicken displays an on-screen version of the report.

Once a report is on-screen, you can check out the details. Move the cursor over the part of the report you'd like to know more about. If the cursor turns into a magnifying glass, you can double-click the mouse to get a QuickZoom Report that scrutinizes your finances even closer.

More Stuff

You can customize the Investment Performance report, memorize it, copy it to the Windows Clipboard, print it, and close its report window in the same way you do a portfolio-value report. (See Reports➪Investment➪Portfolio Value.)

Reports➪Investment➪Capital Gains

The Reports➪Investment➪Capital Gains command opens the Create Report dialog box to the Investment tab. This command also fills in the Report Dates to produce a report that calculates the realized capital gains and losses stemming from the taxable portion of your investment portfolio for a specified interval of time. See also the Reports➪Investment➪Portfolio Value command.

How You Use It

When you choose the Reports➪Investment➪Capital Gains command, Quicken displays the Investment tab of the Create Report dialog box. Use the Report Dates drop-down list box and the from and to boxes to describe the time interval for which you want capital gains and losses calculated. Then choose the Capital Gains button or click Create. Quicken displays an on-screen version of the report.

More Stuff

You can customize the capital gains report, memorize it, copy it to the Windows Clipboard, print it, and close its report window in the same way you do a portfolio-value report. (See Reports➪Investment➪Portfolio Value.)

You can export the capital gains and losses information to a tax export file by selecting the button with an arrow on it and filling in the boxes on the dialog box Quicken displays. Leave the dialog box's List File of Type box set to Tax export files (*.txf) so that Quicken exports the file in a format that a tax-preparation program, such as TurboTax, can easily use.

Reports⇨Investment⇨Investment Income

The Reports⇨Investment⇨Investment Income command opens the Create Report dialog box to the Investment tab. This command also fills in the dialog box to produce a report that summarizes investment income and expense by category for a specified interval of time. See also the Reports⇨Investment⇨Portfolio Value command.

How You Use It

When you choose the Reports⇨Investment⇨Investment Income command, Quicken displays the Investment tab of the Create Report dialog box. Use the Report Dates drop-down list box and the from and to boxes to describe the time interval for which you want investment income and expense summarized. Then choose the Investment Income button or click Create. Quicken displays an on-screen version of the report.

More Stuff

You can customize the Investment Income report, memorize it, copy it to the Windows Clipboard, print it, and close its report window in the same way you do a portfolio-value report. (See Reports⇨Investment⇨Portfolio Value.)

Reports⇨Investment⇨Investment Transactions

The Reports⇨Investment⇨Investment Transactions command opens the Create Report dialog box to the Investment tab. This command also fills in the Report Dates to produce a report that lists your investment transactions for a specific interval of time. See also Reports⇨Investment⇨Portfolio Value.

How You Use It

When you choose the Reports⇨Investment⇨Investment Transactions command, Quicken displays the Investment tab of the Create Report dialog box. Use the Report Dates drop-down list box and the from and to boxes to specify the time interval for which you want investment transactions listed. When you choose the Investment Transactions button or click Create, Quicken displays an on-screen version of the report.

More Stuff

You can customize the Investment Transactions report, memorize it, copy it to the Windows Clipboard, print it, and close its report window in the same way you do a portfolio-value report. (See Reports⇨Investment⇨Portfolio Value.)

Reports⇨Business⇨P&L Statement

The Reports⇨Business⇨P&L Statement command opens the Create Report dialog box to the Business tab and highlights the P&L Statement selection. This command also fills in the Report Dates to produce a report of your year-to-date income and expenses summarized by category. Unlike the business cash-flow reports, which include only transactions from bank accounts and credit card accounts, the business profit-and-loss (P&L) report includes transactions from all accounts.

How You Use It

When you choose the Reports⇨Business⇨P&L Statement command, Quicken displays the Business tab of the Create Report dialog box. Use the Report Dates drop-down list boxes and the from and to boxes to describe the time interval for which you want to calculate profits or losses. Choose the P&L Statement button or click Create to direct Quicken to display an on-screen version of the report.

More Stuff

To print the on-screen version of the report, select the Print command button. Quicken displays the Print Report dialog box. Use its Print to and other options to indicate how Quicken should print the report. Then select OK.

To close the report window, select the Close command button.

You can customize the cash-flow report in all sorts of ways by selecting the Customize command button on the Create Report dialog box or the Customize command button at the top of the Profit & Loss Statement window. Either way, Quicken displays a dialog box you can use to describe how you want the report to appear.

You can have Quicken memorize a business profit-and-loss report by selecting the Memorize command button, which appears at the top of the Profit & Loss Statement window.

You can copy a report to the Windows Clipboard by selecting the Copy command button. You might choose this command to move a report to a spreadsheet program, such as Microsoft Excel.

Finally, to print the report, simply click the Print button and fill in the dialog box.

 Once a report is on-screen, you can check out the details. Move the cursor over the part of the report you'd like to know more about. If the cursor turns into a magnifying glass, you can double-click the mouse to get a QuickZoom Report that scrutinizes your finances even closer.

Reports⇨Business⇨P&L Comparison

The Reports⇨Business⇨P&L Comparison command opens the Create Report dialog box to the Business tab. This command also fills in the Comparison Dates to produce a report of your year-to-date income and expenses summarized by category and your month-to-date income and expenses summarized by category. This report differs from the regular P&L statement in that it allows you to compare profits or losses between two periods of time. See also the Reports⇨Business⇨P&L Statement command.

How You Use It

When you choose the Reports⇨Business⇨P&L Comparison command, Quicken displays the Business tab of the Create Report dialog box and highlights the P&L Comparison selection. Fill in the Compare boxes to specify the time intervals you want to compare. Then choose the P&L Statement button or click Create. Quicken displays an on-screen version of the report.

More Stuff

You can customize the business P&L comparison report, memorize it, copy it to the Windows Clipboard, print it, and close its report window in the same way you do for the profit-and-loss statement. (See Reports⇨Business⇨P&L Statement.)

Reports⇨Business⇨Cash Flow

The Reports⇨Business⇨Cash Flow command opens the Create Report dialog box to the Business tab. This command also fills in the Report Dates to produce a report of transactions from your bank accounts and credit card accounts summarized by income and expense categories. See also the Reports⇨Business⇨P&L Statement command.

How You Use It

When you choose the Reports⇨Business⇨Cash Flow command, Quicken displays the Business tab of the Create Report dialog box. Use the Report Dates drop-down list box and the from and to boxes to describe the time interval you want to summarize. Then choose the Cash Flow button or click Create. Quicken displays an on-screen version of the report.

More Stuff

You can customize the Business CashFlow report, memorize it, copy it to the Windows Clipboard, print it, and close its report window in the same way you do a profit-and-loss statement. (See Reports⇨Business⇨P&L Statement.)

Reports⇨Business⇨A/P by Vendor

The Reports⇨Business⇨A/P by Vendor command opens the Create Report dialog box to the Business tab. This command also fills in the Report Dates to produce a report summarizing the unprinted checks by payee. If you enter unprinted checks for the amounts you owe vendors, this report of unprinted checks describes what you owe vendors — your *accounts payable*. See also the Reports⇨Business⇨P&L Statement command.

How You Use It

When you choose the Reports⇨Business⇨A/P by Vendor command, Quicken displays the Business tab of the Create Report dialog box and highlights the A/P by Vendor selection. Use the Report Dates drop-down list boxes and the from and to boxes to specify the time interval for which you want to summarize unprinted checks. When you choose the A/P by Vendor button or click Create, Quicken displays an on-screen version of the report.

More Stuff

You can customize the A/P by Vendor report, memorize it, copy it to the Windows Clipboard, print it, and close its report window in the same way you do a profit-and-loss statement. (See Reports⇨Business⇨P&L Statement.)

Reports⇨Business⇨A/R by Customer

The Reports⇨Business⇨A/R by Customer command opens the Create Report dialog box to the Business tab. This command also fills in the Report Dates to produce a report summarizing the transactions by payee in the other specified asset accounts. The idea here is that, if you use another asset account for listing customer invoices and payments (or only for listing customer invoices), you can sort of, almost, kind of track your customer invoices this way. Sometimes. See also the Reports⇨Business⇨P&L Statement command.

How You Use It

To track customer receivables within Quicken, you first need to set up another asset account. Enter customer invoices as increases in the account balance. Then, whenever a customer pays some amount, mark the transaction as cleared.

When you want to produce a summary of the uncleared transactions in your other asset account — in other words, your unpaid customer invoices — choose the Reports⇨Business⇨A/R by Customer command. When you choose this command, Quicken displays the Business tab of the Create Report dialog box and highlights the A/R by Customer selection. Use the Report Dates drop-down list box and the from and to boxes to specify the time interval for which you want to summarize uncleared customer invoices. When you choose the A/R by Customer button or click Create, Quicken displays an on-screen version of the report.

If you can't see the A/R by Customer button because report samples appear on the right side of the dialog box, click the Show Report Sample check box to remove the sample reports and expose the A/R by Customer button.

More Stuff

You can customize the A/R by Customer report, memorize it, copy it to the Windows Clipboard, print it, and close its report window in the same way you do a profit-and-loss statement. (See the Reports⇨Business⇨P&L Statement command.)

To specify which accounts get summarized in your A/R by Customer report, select the Customize button on the Create Report dialog box. When Quicken displays the Customize A/R by Customer dialog box, click the Accounts tab. When Quicken displays its list box of accounts, mark the accounts you want Quicken to include on the report and click OK.

Reports⇨Business⇨Job/Project

The Reports⇨Business⇨Job/Project command opens the Create Report dialog box to the Business tab. This command also fills in the Report Dates to produce a report that summarizes income and expense category totals by class. See also the Reports⇨Business⇨P&L Statement command.

How You Use It

To use this report, you first need to set up classes — such as by using the Lists⇨Class command. Then you need to start entering classes — along with categories — when you record income and expense transactions. You enter class names in the category field of the Register window and the Write Checks window following the category name. Separate the category name and the class name with a slash (/).

When you want to produce a summary of the income and expense category totals by class, choose the Reports⇨Business⇨Job/Project command. When you choose this command, Quicken displays the Business tab of the Create Report dialog box and highlights the Job/Project selection. Use the Report Dates drop-down list box and the from and to boxes to specify the time interval for which you want to classify income and expense category totals. When you choose the Job/Project button or click Create, Quicken displays an on-screen version of the report.

If you can't see the Job/Project button because report samples appear on the right side of the dialog box, click the Show Report Sample check box to remove the sample reports and expose the Job/Project button.

More Stuff

You can customize the Job/Project report, memorize it, copy it to the Windows Clipboard, print it, and close its report window in the same way you do a profit-and-loss statement. (See the Reports⇨Business⇨P&L Statement command.)

Reports⇨Business⇨Payroll

The Reports⇨Business⇨Payroll command opens the Create Report dialog box to the Business tab. This command also fills in the Report Dates to produce a report that summarizes transactions you've assigned to the Payroll category. See also the Reports⇨Business⇨P&L Statement command.

How You Use It

As a practical matter, to use this report, you need to use a category named Payroll to summarize all your payroll transactions. If you use the QuickPay add-on utility provided by Quicken, you're already doing this.

When you want to produce a summary of the income and expense category totals by class, choose the Reports⇨Business⇨Payroll command. When you choose this command, Quicken displays the Business tab of the Create Report dialog box and highlights the Payroll selection. Use the Report Dates drop-down list box and the from and to boxes to specify the time interval for which you want to summarize payroll transactions. Probably you'll want to choose the most recent quarter or calendar year. When you choose OK, Quicken displays an on-screen version of the report.

If you can't see the Payroll button because report samples appear on the right side of the dialog box, click the Show Report Sample check box to remove the sample reports and expose the Payroll button.

More Stuff

You can customize the Payroll report, memorize it, copy it to the Windows Clipboard, print it, and close its report window in the same way you do a profit-and-loss statement. (See the Reports⇨Business⇨P&L Statement command.)

Reports⇨Business⇨Balance Sheet

The Reports⇨Business⇨Balance Sheet command opens the Create Report dialog box to the Business tab. This command also fills in the dialog box to produce a report that lists account balances as of a specified date.

To produce a reasonably accurate balance-sheet report, you need to have already set up accounts for all your assets and liabilities. You also need to have been keeping accurate records for these assets and liabilities. One other thing I should briefly mention here is that Quicken doesn't describe the nitty-gritty details of your owner's equity, even though technically it's supposed to. It just calculates the difference between your total assets and your total liabilities. See also the Reports⇨Business⇨P&L Statement command.

How You Use It

When you choose the Reports⇨Business⇨Balance Sheet command, Quicken displays the Business tab of the Create Report dialog box and highlights the Balance Sheet selection. Use the Report Balance as of list box to specify the date for which Quicken will report account balances. When you choose the Balance Sheet button or click Create, Quicken displays an on-screen version of the report.

If you can't see the Balance Sheet button because report samples appear on the right side of the dialog box, click the Show Report Sample check box to remove the sample reports and expose the Balance Sheet button.

More Stuff

You can customize the Balance Sheet report, memorize it, copy it to the Windows Clipboard, print it, and close its report window in the same way you do for a profit-and-loss statement. (See Reports⇨Business⇨P&L Statement.)

Reports⇨Business⇨Missing Checks

The Reports⇨Business⇨Missing Checks command opens the Create Report dialog box to the Business tab. This command also fills in the dialog box to produce a report that lists transactions in order of check number and highlights gaps in the check number sequence. Just in case you're wondering, yes, this business report is identical to the missing checks report you can create with the Reports⇨Home⇨Missing Checks command. See also the Reports⇨Business⇨P&L Statement command.

How You Use It

When you choose the Reports⇨Business⇨Missing Checks command, Quicken displays the Business tab of the Create Report dialog box. If you can't see the Missing Checks selection, click the down-arrow on the scroll bar to scroll down to that selection. Use the Report Dates drop-down list boxes and the from and to boxes to specify the time interval for which Quicken should list transactions and flag check-numbering gaps. When you select the Missing Checks button or click Create, Quicken displays an on-screen version of the report.

More Stuff

You can customize the Missing Checks report, memorize it, copy it to the Windows Clipboard, print it, and close its report window in the same way you do a profit-and-loss statement. (See Reports⇨Business⇨P&L Statement.)

Reports⇨Business⇨Comparison

The Reports⇨Business⇨Comparison command opens the Create Report dialog box to the Business tab. This command also fills in the Compare Dates to produce a report that compares income and expense category totals for two time intervals — such as last year's totals and this year's totals. Yes, this business report is identical to the Home Comparison report you can create with the Reports⇨Home⇨Comparison command. See also Reports⇨ Business⇨P&L Statement.

How You Use It

When you choose the Reports⇨Business⇨Comparison command, Quicken displays the Business tab of the Create Report dialog box. If you can't see the Comparison selection, click the down-arrow on the scroll bar to scroll down to that selection. Fill in the Compare Dates to specify the time intervals for which Quicken should make the comparison. Then choose the Comparison button or click Create to have Quicken display an on-screen version of the report.

More Stuff

You can customize the Comparison report, memorize it, copy it to the Windows Clipboard, print it, and close its report window in the same way you do a profit-and-loss statement. (See Reports⇨Business⇨P&L Statement.)

Reports⇨Other⇨Transaction

The Reports⇨Other⇨Transaction command opens the Create Report dialog box to the Other tab. This command also fills in the Report dates to produce a report that lists the transactions in the active account.

Actually, you don't need to use this report. Almost anytime you want to print a list of transactions, you can use one of the home, investment, or business reports that list transactions.

How You Use It

When you choose the Reports⇨Other⇨Transaction command, Quicken displays the Other tab of the Create Report dialog box and highlights the Transaction selection. Use the Report Dates drop-down list box and the from and to boxes to specify the time interval for which you want to list transactions. Choose the Transaction button or click Create to direct Quicken to display an on-screen version of the report.

More Stuff

You can customize the Transaction report, memorize it, copy it to the Windows Clipboard, print it, and close its report window in the same way you do other reports. (See Reports⇨Business⇨P&L Statement.)

Reports⇨Other⇨Summary

The Reports⇨Other⇨Summary command opens the Create Report dialog box to the Other tab. This command also fills in the Report Dates to produce a report that summarizes account information — usually by totaling income and expense categories.

You actually don't need to use this report. Almost anytime you want to print a summary of transactions, you can use one of the Home, Investment, or Business submenu reports that summarize account information.

How You Use It

When you choose the Reports⇨Other⇨Summary command, Quicken displays the Other tab of the Create Report dialog box and highlights the Summary selection. Use the Report Dates drop-down list box and the from and to boxes to specify the time interval for which you want to summarize transactions. Choose the Summary button or click Create to direct Quicken to display an on-screen version of the report.

More Stuff

You can customize the Summary report, memorize it, copy it to the Windows Clipboard, print it, and close its report window in the same way you do other reports. (See Reports⇨Business⇨P&L Statement.)

Reports⇨Other⇨Comparison

The Reports⇨Other⇨Comparison command opens the Create Report dialog box to the Other tab. This command also fills in the Compare Dates to produce a report that compares category totals for two time intervals.

Actually, you don't need to use this report. You can use the Home or Business submenu's comparison report.

How You Use It

When you choose the Reports⇨Other⇨Comparison command, Quicken displays the Other tab of the Create Report dialog box and highlights the Comparison selection. Fill in the Compare Dates to specify the time intervals for which Quicken should make the comparison. Then choose the Comparison button or click Create to have Quicken display an on-screen version of the report.

More Stuff

You can customize the Comparison report, memorize it, copy it to the Windows Clipboard, print it, and close its report window in the same way you do other reports. (See Reports⇨Business⇨P&L Statement.)

Reports⇨Other⇨Budget

The Reports⇨Other⇨Budget command opens the Create Report dialog box to the Other tab. This command also fills in the Report Dates to produce a report that compares your budget to your year-to-date income and expenses summarized by category. A budget report that you produce by using the Reports⇨Other⇨Budget command is essentially the same as the one you can produce by using the Reports⇨Home⇨Monthly Budget command. See also the Plan⇨Budgeting command.

How You Use It

To produce a budget report, you first need to set up a budget by using the Plan⇨Budgeting command. Once you've completed this prerequisite, choose the Reports⇨Other⇨Budget command. When you do, Quicken displays the Other tab of the Create Report dialog box and highlights the Budget selection. Use the Report Dates drop-down list box and the from and to boxes to describe the time interval for which you want to compare actual and budgeted amounts. Then choose the Budget button or click Create. Quicken displays an on-screen version of the report.

More Stuff

You can customize the Budget report, memorize it, copy it to the Windows Clipboard, print it, and close its report window in the same way you do other reports. (See Reports⇨Business⇨P&L Statement.)

Reports⇨Other⇨Account Balances

The Reports⇨Other⇨Account Balances command opens the Create Report dialog box to the Other tab. This command also fills in the Report Balance as of box to produce a report that lists account balances as of a specified date.

The account balances report, by the way, is the same report as the home net-worth report and the business balance-sheet report. All are account balances reports.

How You Use It

When you choose the Reports⇨Other⇨Account Balances command, Quicken displays the Other tab of the Create Report dialog box and highlights the Account Balances selection. Use the Report Balance as of drop-down list box to specify the date for which Quicken will report account balances. When you choose the Account Balances button or click Create, Quicken displays an on-screen version of the report.

More Stuff

You can customize an Account Balances report, memorize it, copy it to the Windows Clipboard, print it, and close its report window in the same way you do other reports. (See Reports⇨Business⇨P&L Statement.)

Reports⇨Memorized Reports

The Reports⇨Memorized Reports command opens Create Report dialog box to the Memorized tab. This dialog box lists the reports you've memorized and, presumably, will use time and time again.

How You Use It

You need to memorize a report or two before you can begin printing memorized reports. This makes sense, right? To memorize a report, click the Memorize command button, which appears along the top edge of the report window. Quicken displays a dialog box that asks you to name the report and, optionally, to provide a report date range.

After you've memorized a report, you can use it by choosing the Reports⇨Memorized Reports command. When you choose this command, Quicken displays the Memorized tab of the Create Reports dialog box. Select the memorized report and then the Use command button.

More Stuff

The Memorized Reports window also provides two additional command buttons: Edit and Delete. Edit lets you rename the memorized report. Delete deletes the memorized report.

Reports⇨Graphs⇨Income and Expense

The Reports⇨Graphs⇨Income and Expense command opens the Create Graph dialog box and selects the Income and Expense Graph option button. You use this command to display a bar graph that plots monthly income and expense totals.

How You Use It

When you choose the Reports⇨Graphs⇨Income and Expense command, Quicken displays the Create Graph dialog box. Use the From and To boxes to specify the time interval for which you want to plot monthly income and monthly expense totals. Then choose Create. Quicken provides the graph.

If you have a question about some piece of data you see plotted — one of the income bars, for example — move the cursor over the data. When the cursor turns into a magnifying glass, double-click to tell Quicken that you want to use QuickZoom to zoom in on the data marker. Quicken then displays a QuickZoom graph that further explains the data. You can even use QuickZoom to zoom in on a QuickZoom graph, but, in this case, Quicken displays a report that explains the data.

Steps

❶

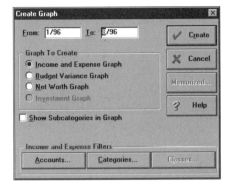

❷

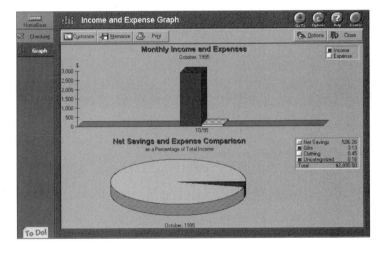

❸

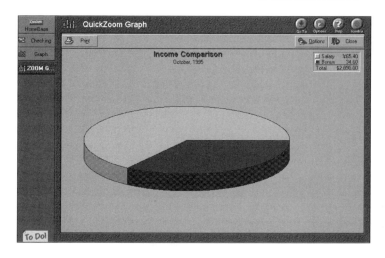

❹

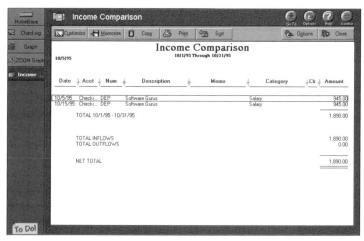

More Stuff

At the bottom of the Create Graph dialog box are three command
buttons you can use to *filter,* or control, which data gets plotted:
Accounts, Categories, and Classes. Each of the command buttons
works in roughly the same way. You click the command buttons
to display a list of accounts, categories, or classes. Then you use
the list to indicate which accounts, categories, or classes you
want to appear.

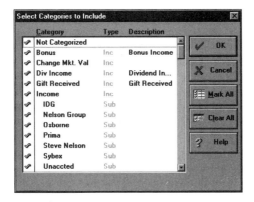

The Reports⇨Graphs⇨Budget Variance command opens the Create Graph dialog box and selects the Budget Variance Graph option button. You use this command to display a bar graph that plots budgeted and actual monthly net income and that plots budgeted and actual category totals. See also the Reports⇨ Graphs⇨Income and Expense command.

How You Use It

When you choose the Reports⇨Graphs⇨Budget Variance command, Quicken displays the Create Graph dialog box. Use the From and To boxes to specify the time interval for which you want to plot actual and budgeted monthly income and expense totals. Then choose Create. Quicken provides the graph.

More Stuff

You can filter the data provided to a budget variance graph and use QuickZoom to zoom in on its data markers in the same way you filter and use QuickZoom with an income-and-expense graph. (See Reports⇨Graphs⇨Income and Expense.)

Reports⇨Graphs⇨Net Worth

The Reports⇨Graphs⇨Net Worth command opens the Create
Graph dialog box and selects the Net Worth Graph option button.
You use this command to display a bar graph that plots asset and
liability account balances and the difference between the two,
which is your *net worth*. See also the Reports⇨Graphs⇨Income
and Expense Graph command.

How You Use It

When you choose the Reports⇨Graphs⇨Net Worth command,
Quicken displays the Create Graph dialog box. Use the From and
To boxes to describe the time interval for which you want to plot
account balances and your net worth. Then choose Create.
Quicken provides the graph.

More Stuff

You can use QuickZoom to zoom in on a Net Worth graph's data
markers in the same way you use QuickZoom with an income-and-
expense graph. (See Reports⇨Graphs⇨Income and Expense.)

Reports⇨Graphs⇨Investments

The Reports⇨Graphs⇨Investments command opens the Create
Graph dialog box and selects the Investment Graph option
button. You use this command to display a bar graph that plots
the monthly value of your investment portfolio and a bar graph
that plots the average annual return of each of the securities in
your investment portfolio. See also the Reports⇨Graphs⇨Income
and Expense command.

How You Use It

When you choose the Reports⇨Graphs⇨Investments command,
Quicken displays the Create Graph dialog box. Use the From and
To boxes to specify the time interval you want to plot investment
portfolio values and average annual returns for securities. Then
choose Create. Quicken provides the graph.

More Stuff

By default, the investment graph shows investment values and average annual returns by security. You can use the Type, Goal, Sec, and Account command buttons to change this format, however. Choose Type, for example, to show investment values and average annual returns by investment type. Or choose Goal or Account to show investment values and average annual returns by investment goal or account, respectively. Use the Sec command button to switch back to the default display by security.

As with the other graphs, you can use QuickZoom to zoom in on an investment graph's data markers. (See, for example, Reports⇨Graphs⇨Income and Expense.)

Reports⇨Memorized Graphs

The Reports⇨Memorized Graphs command opens the Memorized Graphs dialog box. From this dialog box, you can choose a graph you've memorized, click Use, and make your graph appear on-screen.

How You Use It

All the Graph windows have a Memorize button that you can click to make Quicken memorize a graph. When you click the Memorize button, a dialog box comes on-screen so you can give the graph a memorable name. You enter the name and click OK, at which point Quicken remembers what your graph looks like. Usually, you memorize a graph when you've customized it somehow or other, and you don't want to have to go through the business of customizing a graph in the same way ever again.

Choose the Reports⇨Memorized Graphs command to find and look at a graph that Quicken has memorized. In the Memorized Graphs dialog box, click the graph and click the Use button. The

Recall Memorized Graph dialog box appears. Here's a chance to fool with the graph even more, if you want to. More likely, though, you'll just click OK. Your graph appears on-screen.

More Stuff

You can change the name of a memorized graph. Click its name in the Memorized Graphs dialog box and click Edit. Then enter a new name in the Edit Memorized Graph dialog box.

If you want to delete a graph, select it and press the Delete button.

Reports➪*Snapshots*

The Reports➪Snapshots command attempts, in one fell swoop, to give you a glimpse of your entire financial picture — where your expenses are, your monthly income and expenses, your net worth, whether you have met your budget goals, your portfolio, and any notes you've made to yourself in the current calendar period.

How You Use It

To try out this all-encompassing command, either choose Reports➪Snapshots or click the SnpShts icon, the one that shows a camera, on the iconbar. After a short lull, you see the six-part screen with the six *snapshots* on it. Happy viewing!

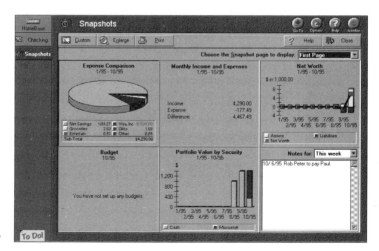

More Stuff

Notice the row of buttons along the top of the Snapshots window? Click on one of the snapshots and click the E_n_large button if you want to see a close-up of some area of your finances. When you click E_n_large, you see a standard graph window with all the amenities you find in normal graph windows.

The _P_rint button — well, you get the idea.

Click _C_ustom if you want to see fewer than six or more than six snapshots in the Snapshots window. You can also decide which areas of your financial picture appear in the Snapshots window.

Reports ➪ Reconciliation

The _R_eports ➪ _R_econciliation command opens the Reconciliation Report Setup dialog box. You use this command to produce a bank account reconciliation report if you now want one but forgot to print one the last time you reconciled a bank account. See also the Acti_v_ities ➪ _R_econcile command.

How You Use It

Open the register for which you want a Reconciliation report and choose the _R_eports ➪ _R_econciliation command. Enter a report title if you want one. Use the _B_ank Balance as of box to indicate the bank-statement closing date. Use the Transactions to Include option buttons — All Transactions and Summary and Uncleared — to indicate how much detail you want on the reconciliation report. Then choose _P_rint.

Quicken displays the Print Report dialog box. Use its Print to and other options to indicate how Quicken should print the report. Then choose OK.

Steps

❶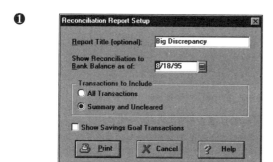

❷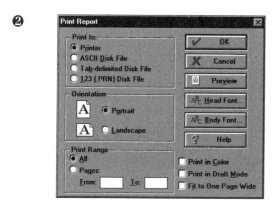

Plan Menu Commands

The Plan menu provides tools for personal financial planning and
budgeting. You don't need to use any of the Plan menu commands
in your daily financial record-keeping. So it's all too easy to ignore
them, forget about them, or never use them. Try not to fall into
this trap, however. I think these are probably Quicken's most
valuable tools.

Plan⇨Budgeting

You can *budget,* or plan, what the monthly and annual category totals should be. Before you grab your ears and run into the other room screaming, let me point out that, if you do budget, you'll benefit in two ways.

- First benefit: You'll be able to make sure that your income and outgo are balanced. (This generally leads to good things — such as less stress and greater marital harmony.)

- Second benefit: You'll be able to monitor your spending as the year rolls along.

See also the Reports⇨Home⇨Monthly Budget and Reports⇨ Other⇨Budget commands.

How You Use It

After you've set up your categories, you're ready to rock and roll. Choose the Plan⇨Budgeting command. Quicken displays the Budget window, which is a spreadsheet. The spreadsheet columns show months, and the spreadsheet rows show income and expense categories. You budget the category totals by month by entering amounts into the column/row intersections.

Category View	Jan	Feb	Mar	Apr	May	Totals
INFLOWS						
◆ Bonus	100	0	100	0	0	200
◆ Div Income	250	250	250	0	0	750
◆ Gift Received	0	0	0	0	0	0
◆ Int Inc	0	0	0	0	0	0
◆ Invest Inc	55	55	55	0	0	165
◆ Online Data Inc	45	45	45	0	0	135
◆ Other Inc	0	0	0	0	0	0
◆ Salary	1900	1900	1900	0	0	5700
◆ Salary Spouse	1250	1250	1250	0	0	3750
◆ _DivInc	0	0	0	0	0	0
◆ _IntInc	0	0	0	0	0	0
◆ _LT CapGnDst	0	0	0	0	0	0
◆ _RlzdGain	0	0	0	0	0	0
◆ _ST CapGnDst	0	0	0	0	0	0
◆ _UnrlzdGain	0	0	0	0	0	0
OUTFLOWS						
Auto	0	0	0	0	0	0
Total Inflows	3600	3500	3600	0	0	10700
Total Outflows	0	0	0	0	0	0
Difference	3600	3500	3600	0	0	10700

More Stuff

At the top of the Budget window is a row of buttons. Because we're already on the subject of budgets, let me you give you the 10-cent tour and describe what these buttons do.

- Budgets displays a dialog box that lets you choose another budget, if you've created more than one. Choose another budget from the Manage Budgets dialog box and click Open to see and work with it. You can also create new budgets from this dialog box.

- The button that shows a pencil and a red tapeworm is the Edit button. It displays a short menu of commands that lets you erase rows or copy the current cell's budget to the right (into future months), or down (into other categories).

- Layout displays a dialog box you can use to tell Quicken how you want the budget spreadsheet to be set up — for example, whether to budget monthly, quarterly, or annually.

- Print, in a surprise turn of events, prints the budget spreadsheet you see on your screen.

- Save saves the budget to disk. (You don't name the budget.)

- Restore lets you retrieve the version of the budget that you last saved.

- Close closes the Budget window.

Plan⇨Forecasting

The Plan⇨Forecasting command lets you forecast future account balances — such as your bank account balance — on the basis of scheduled transactions and averages from the past.

How You Use It

Choose the Plan⇨Forecasting command. When Quicken displays the Automatically Create Forecast dialog box, specify a date range in the past that Quicken should use to predict the future.

If you want to get real fancy, you can click the Advanced button and use the Advanced AutoCreate dialog box's radio buttons to specify whether Quicken uses scheduled transactions or estimates based on the budget and register data.

When you go back to the Automatically Create Forecast dialog box and click OK, Quicken displays the Forecasting window.

Steps

❶

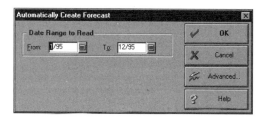

❷

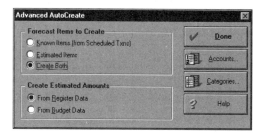

❸

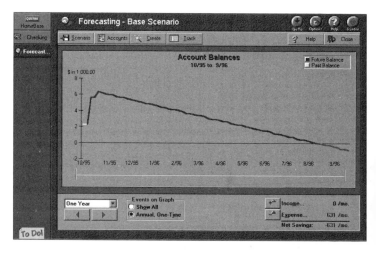

More Stuff

- Click the Scenario button to name and save your forecasts.

- Click the Accounts button to display the Select Accounts to Include dialog box. Mysteriously, this button lets you select for which accounts Quicken should forecast balances.

- Click the Create button to redisplay the Automatically Create Forecast dialog box. (You might do this so that you can change the forecasting method.)

- Click the Track button to do some budgeting based on the forecast.

You can also click the Income and Expense buttons in the lower right corner of the window to display dialog boxes that let you forecast income and expense items by supercategory, category, and subcategory.

Plan⇨Financial Planners⇨Loan

Choose the Plan⇨Financial Planners⇨Loan command to display the Loan Planner dialog box. This dialog box lets you calculate outstanding loan balances and loan payments.

How You Use It

To use the Loan Planner (after you've chosen this command, of course), first use the Calculate option buttons to indicate what it is you want to calculate: the loan amount or the payment. Then fill in the Loan Information text boxes with whatever data you already know.

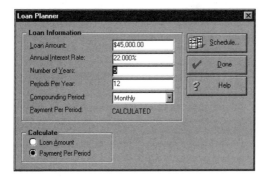

More Stuff

Select the Schedule command button to display an amortization schedule that shows loan balances and the interest and principal portions of loan payments. The amortization-schedule dialog box includes a Print command button so that you can print a copy of the amortization schedule.

Plan⇨Financial Planners⇨Savings

Choose the Plan⇨Financial Planners⇨Savings command to display the Investment Savings Planner dialog box. This dialog box lets you perform compound-interest calculations — such as how fast your savings will grow. This Financial Planner also lets you include (or exclude) the effect of inflation on your savings.

How You Use It

To use the Investment Savings Planner, first use the Calculate option buttons to indicate what it is you want to calculate: the opening savings balance, the regular (or *periodic*) contribution you'll save, or the ending savings balance. Then fill in the Savings Information text boxes.

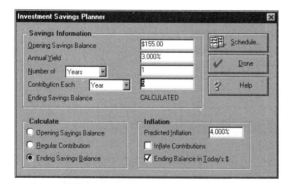

More Stuff

To include or exclude the effects of inflation, use the Inflation boxes. You can enter your estimate of future inflation in the Predicted Inflation text box. Mark the Inflate Contributions check box if you'll increase your savings over time as inflation occurs.

Mark the Ending Balance In Today's $ check box if you want the ending savings balance to show current-day, uninflated dollars instead of future, inflated dollars.

If you calculate the regular contribution (*periodic savings*) amount, you can select the Schedule command button to display a deposit schedule that shows savings balances, regular contributions, and interest income over the years you save.

Plan⇨Financial Planners⇨College

Choose the Plan⇨Financial Planners⇨College command to display the College Planner dialog box. Not only does the College Planner allow you to plan for a child's (or grandchild's) college costs, it's also guaranteed to trigger a series of bad dreams concerning Junior's or Little Missy's future.

How You Use It

To use the College Planner, select Plan⇨Financial Planners⇨ College and use the Calculate option buttons to indicate what it is you want to calculate: the annual college costs, the amount you should have already saved, or the annual amount you'll need to save each year from now on until college graduation. Then fill in the College Information text boxes.

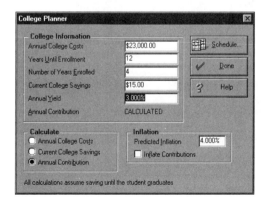

More Stuff

To include or exclude the effects of inflation, use the Inflation boxes. You can enter your estimate of future inflation in the Predicted Inflation text box. Mark the Inflate Contributions check box if you'll increase your savings over time as inflation occurs.

Select the Schedule command button to display a deposit schedule that shows college savings balances, annual savings, and tuition withdrawals.

Plan⇨Financial Planners⇨Retirement

Choose the Plan⇨Financial Planners⇨Retirement command to display the Retirement Planner dialog box. This dialog box lets you calculate how much you need to save if you hope someday to retire.

How You Use It

To use the Retirement Planner, choose Plan⇨Financial Planners⇨Retirement and use the Calculate option buttons to indicate what it is you want to calculate: the amount you should have already saved for retirement, the annual amount you should save for the rest of your employment years, or the annual retirement income you'll enjoy given your current and planned savings. Then fill in the Retirement Information text boxes.

Retirement Planner

Retirement Information

Current Savings	$10,000.00
Annual Yield	8.000%
Annual Contribution	$3,000.00
Current Age	37
Retirement Age	75
Withdraw Until Age	85
Other Income (SSI, etc.)	$0.00
Annual Income After Taxes	CALCULATED

Schedule...

Done

Help

Tax Information

○ Tax Sheltered Investment   Current Tax Rate   28.000%
● Non-Sheltered Investment   Retirement Tax Rate   15.000%

Calculate

○ Current Savings
○ Annual Contribution
● Annual Retirement Income

Inflation

Predicted Inflation   2.000%
☐ Inflate Contributions
☑ Annual Income in Today's $

More Stuff

If you want to experiment with the effects of income taxes on your retirement savings, you'll learn something you probably already know. Tax-sheltered investments such as 401(k)s, 403(b)s, and Individual Retirement Accounts IRAs are too good to pass up.

To include or exclude the effects of inflation — and you should definitely take inflation into account — use the Inflation boxes. You can enter your estimate of future inflation in the Predicted Inflation text box. Mark the Inflate Contributions check box if you'll increase your savings over time as inflation occurs. Mark the Annual Income In Today's $ if you want to denominate your retirement income in current-day, uninflated dollars.

Select the Schedule command button to display a deposit schedule that shows retirement savings balances, annual savings, and annual withdrawals.

Plan⇨Financial Planners⇨Refinance

Choose the Plan⇨Financial Planners⇨Refinance command to display the Refinance Planner dialog box. This dialog box lets you calculate how long it takes for you to recover your refinancing costs because you've lowered your payments.

How You Use It

To use the Refinance Planner, you choose this command and then fill in the text boxes. Quicken uses this information to make several calculations, including the new monthly mortgage payment and the number of months it takes to break even. For example, if it costs $2,000 to refinance, and you'll save $100 a month, the Refinance Planner tells you it takes 20 months to recover your refinancing costs (20 months times $100 equals $2,000).

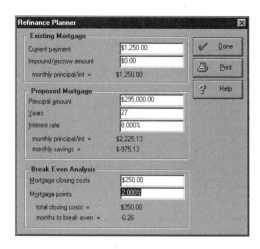

More Stuff

A word to the wise: Don't use the Refinance Planner to determine whether or not it makes financial sense to refinance a mortgage. Sorry, but it doesn't do that. The Refinance Planner only tells you how long it takes to recover the cost of refinancing through lower monthly payments.

By the way, if you truly want to save money by refinancing, you need to do two things. You need to lower your interest costs by making sure the annual percentage rate (which includes the interest plus the refinancing costs) on the new loan is less than the interest rate on the current loan. And you need to make sure that, by refinancing, you don't borrow money for a longer period of time. (For example, even in the case where interest rates drop significantly, it probably doesn't make sense to refinance a mortgage with 15 years of payments left if the new mortgage requires 30 years of payments.)

Plan⇨Tax Planner

Use the Plan⇨Tax Planner command to estimate your 1995 or 1996 income-tax expenses.

How You Use It

To use the Tax Planner, first choose this command (of course). Then describe your income-tax situation using the boxes and buttons in the Tax Planner dialog box. You need to do things such as indicate your filing status, pick the right year, and enter information about your income, tax deductions, and tax payments.

If Quicken can collect enough information about income-tax planning with a single, simple text box, you'll see the text box on the Tax Planner window. If Quicken can't collect enough information about income-tax planning with a single, simple text box, you click a button — such as the Interest/Dividend Income button. Then, when Quicken displays a dialog box with a cute, little worksheet, you fill in the worksheet's blanks.

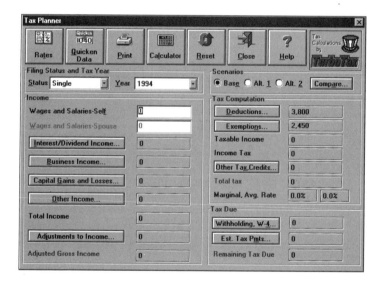

More Stuff

If the income tax-rate schedules change, you can click the Rates button to display a dialog box that lets you update the tax-rate schedules that Quicken uses.

You click the Quicken Data button to have Quicken grab income and deductions data from your Quicken file. (You still need to review all the inputs if you go this route — just in case you need to fill in any missing pieces of the tax puzzle.)

You can click the Print button to print the Tax Planner information.

You probably would not guess as much in a million years, but clicking the Calculator button tells Quicken to display its oh-so-handy calculator.

The Reset button tells Quicken to erase all your inputs so that the Tax Planner inputs look like they did before you started changing stuff.

Click Close when you've had enough.

Plan⇨Savings Goals

Use the Plan⇨Savings Goals command to create wealth accumulation goals you want to monitor. Okay. I'll say right here at the start that I think this whole savings goal thing is a bit kooky. No, I don't think it's bad to have financial goals. Goals are great. But, well, I think you'll see what I mean if you start noodling around. . . .

How You Use It

To create a savings goal, choose the Plan⇨Savings Goals command. Quicken displays the empty Savings Goals window. It's empty because you don't have any savings goals. You can change all that by clicking New.

Quicken displays the Create New Savings Goal dialog box. You fill in the dialog box. When you click OK, Quicken redisplays the Savings Goals window — only this time it shows the new goal. At the bottom of the screen, you see a monthly savings figure. This is the amount you (or I) need to save monthly in order to reach a goal.

Steps

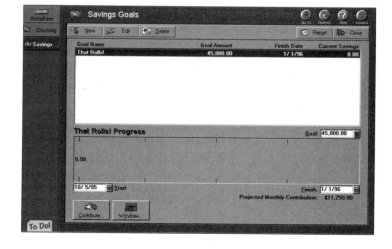

More Stuff

"How," you ask, "does Quicken track your progress in achieving a savings goal?" Okay, here's how this whole thing works. It turns out that savings goals are actually akin to compartments in your other accounts. So, if you do have the goal of buying a Rolls Royce, then every time you have a little extra money to put aside, you transfer the money to the savings goal. No, the money you've "set aside" doesn't actually leave, say, the bank account. (It still shows up when you reconcile the bank account, for example.) But Quicken does adjust the account balance it shows in the register for the effect of your savings-goal transactions.

Plan⇨Progress Bar

Use the Plan⇨Progress Bar command to add to the bottom of the Quicken desktop a bar that shows your progress in achieving a savings goal or meeting some budgeting goal, or that shows a supercategory total.

How You Use It

To add a progress bar, just choose this command. When Quicken displays the Progress Bar dialog box, use its Cust (Customize) button to indicate what you see.

If you decide that you don't want to see the darn thing anymore, click the Close button on the right side of the bar.

The Add-Ons Menu Commands

The Add-Ons menu doesn't really relate to Quicken — or at least not directly. What it does is either start other programs you can buy from Intuit (TurboTax, QuickInvoice or QuickPay) or display advertisements for these other programs (TurboTax, QuickInvoice, or QuickPay) if you haven't yet purchased them. That's pretty much all I can say about the Add-Ons menu commands, so I won't spend any more space describing them.

The Online Menu Commands

The Online menu provides commands you use to connect or monkey with Quicken's online services. Just to make this whole thing painlessly quick, there are really only two true online services: a credit-card statement by modem service (available to people who have the Quicken IntelliCharge credit card) and a securities prices by modem service. Sure, there are a bunch of other commands on the Online menu. But these commands either support one of the two true online services, or these commands are really as much for Intuit's benefit as yours.

Online ⇨ Online Banking

Choose the Online ⇨ Online Banking command to get financial data — such as your current balance and transaction lists from your different accounts — by modem. To use this command, you must have enrolled in the online service. And, needless to say, your bank must offer online services through Quicken.

You might remember seeing the Enable Online Banking check box when you set up a new account. After you've enrolled in the Online Banking service, you go back to the Bank Account Setup dialog box and click that Enable Online Banking check box. Then you can bank online. You must have an Intuit membership to use this command. See Online ⇨ Intuit Membership.

If you went fishing and a fish took the bait, and you were reeling in the fish, could you say you had a "fish online"?

Online ⇨ Online Bill Payment

Choose the Online ⇨ Online Bill Payment command to pay bills electronically. You must have enrolled with the Online Bill Payment service to use this command. To be more precise, you must have enrolled with a financial service that lets you pay bills by modem.

Quicken gives you all the help in the world if paying bills online is what you want to do. See the Help feature for details.

You must have an Intuit membership to use this command. See Online ⇨ Intuit Membership.

Online⇨Portfolio Price Update

Use the Online⇨Portfolio Price Update command to connect to an online service that provides delayed stock, bond, and mutual fund prices for the securities on your securities list. The only thing you need to do to use this command is make sure that, when you set up the security, you gave the correct security symbol, because this symbol is how Quicken identifies and grabs security price information.

If you choose this command, you see the Update Portfolio Prices dialog box. It informs you that the service costs $2.95 per month for six updates of your portfolio. And you get three, count 'em, three free updates.

You must have an Intuit membership to use this command. See Online⇨Intuit Membership.

How You Use It

Just choose this command and click OK in the Update Portfolio Prices dialog box. Quicken displays a message box telling you that it's trying to connect to the computer that provides the stock prices. If Quicken successfully connects, it grabs relatively up-to-date prices for the securities. For the complete lowdown, see the Help files.

More Stuff

The securities prices that Quicken gets aren't up-to-date. They are delayed by at least 15 minutes. (To get immediate prices, you have to get one of the online services that the big boys and big girls use.)

Online⇨Software Registration

You can register your software online using this command. The folks at Intuit, apparently feeling that you have nothing better to do than help their marketing research effort, also want you to provide some information about who you are and how you use Quicken. Nice try guys, but I think I'll pass.

Online⇨Quicken Financial Network

I love going to the movies. What I don't like is this recent trend of showing commercials before the movie starts. Big-screen commercials. You see them and think, "This is one reason I went to the movies in the first place — to get away from commercials."

Choose the Online⇨Quicken Financial Network, and you feel a similar wave of disappointment. On-screen are not one or two, but a dozen computer-screen billboards. Click one of them and you get to see an advertisement. The Chase Bank ad has a prodigious amount of fine print on it. A really prodigious amount.

Online⇨Intuit Marketplace

You can order products and supplies online from Intuit. All you need to do is start the Intuit Marketplace application, which you can do by choosing the Online⇨Intuit Marketplace command. (You can also choose Activities⇨Order Checks to get to the Intuit Marketplace.)

I figure that, because the Intuit Marketplace isn't really part of the Quicken product, and given that it's partly advertisement, that's pretty much all I need to say.

Online➪Intuit Membership

In order to use Quicken's online services, you must have an Intuit membership. This is the command you use to set up a membership, view the information (such as the password) in your membership, and change your membership information.

How You Use It

Choose the Online➪Intuit Membership➪Set up command and click the Set up option. Fill in your intimate personal details and click OK. If you haven't set up your modem yet (with the Online➪Set Up Modem command), Quicken takes a shot at setting up your modem now. I hope it succeeds. If it doesn't, you might have to go to the aforementioned command and monkey around a bit.

When you become a member, you see a message saying as much on-screen. You also get your membership number. This is the number to use if you ever call Intuit for technical support.

More Stuff

If you forget your membership number and need to see it, choose Online➪Intuit Membership➪View Detail.

Online➪Membership Password➪Store

To use most of the online services, you need a password. Use the Online➪Membership Password➪Store command to tuck your password away in a safe place. After you've stored your password, you won't have to enter it to access an online service.

To store a password, choose this command, click a box next to the service or services you're using, and click OK. Then enter your password.

Use the Online⇔Membership Password⇔Change command to change the password you use to connect to online services. As long as you know your current password, there isn't much to using this command. You just choose it and then do what comes naturally. For security reasons, and so that some 12-year-old hacker doesn't get into trouble, I won't go into any more detail than this. If you want more information, check out Quicken's Help files.

Online⇔Set Up Modem

If you want to use any of the online services, just choose this command to have Quicken configure your modem for you. There's nothing to using this command. Quicken does all the work for you. Oh, I should say that you need to turn on your modem before you choose this command. But that's all you need to do.

Window Menu Commands

The first three Window menu commands let you arrange or close the windows and window icons that Quicken displays. But I should point out that these usually aren't the only Window menu commands. Quicken also provides numbered Window menu commands that list the open document windows. You can activate one of these windows by choosing its numbered command.

Window⇔Cascade

The Window⇔Cascade command arranges all the open document windows in a layered stack so that only the title bars are visible on all except the topmost open window, like papers stacked on top of each other, but arranged so that the first line of each page is visible.

How You Use It

You just choose this command. There's nothing tricky, nothing special. Almost all Windows applications, by the way, have a Window⇔Cascade command. It's like the law.

Window⇨Arrange Icons

The Window⇨Arrange Icons command arranges the icons for all the minimized document windows in a neat little row along the button edge of the Quicken application window.

How You Use It

Again, you just choose this command.

By the way, I don't mean to bring up an awkward subject, but if terms such as *icons, minimized document windows,* and *application window* sound like technobabble, you might benefit by learning a bit more about the Windows 95 operating environment. I recommend getting a good book on the subject, like *Windows 95 For Dummies.*

While I'm on the subject, I may as well mention that the aforementioned italicized terms are indeed technobabble.

Window⇨Close All Windows

The Window⇨Close All Windows command removes all the open document windows from the Quicken application.

How You Use It

Just choose it. If it makes you panicky to see all the ornamentation stripped away from the Quicken screen, just click the HomeBse icon. It all comes back.

Help Menu Commands

Quicken's Help menu commands let you start the Windows Help application and open the Quicken Help file. The Quicken Help file, incidentally, is like an online, inside-your-computer user's guide. The feature that makes it pretty darn handy is that you can use the power of your computer to quickly find descriptions of terms, tasks, and techniques.

Help⇨Quicken Help

The Help⇨Quicken Help command starts the Windows Help application and opens the Quicken Help file. All with just a click.

How You Use It

Choose the Help⇨Quicken Help command. Quicken displays a list of help topics related to the window you're working with: how to enter a new transaction, how to change a previous transaction, and so on. You click the topic you want to know more about. Quicken then displays another screen full of information about the whatever you asked to learn more about.

To exit the Help application, choose its File⇨Exit command or click the Close button in the upper-right corner of the window.

More Stuff

This isn't a book about Windows, so I'm not going to beat the Help thing into the ground. I do want to tell you about Search, however. At the top of the Help application window, you'll see a command button labeled Search.

If you select this command button, Help displays the Help Topics dialog box. You use this dialog box to describe the general topic you want help with. Type a noun or verb related to your problem in the text box at the top of the dialog box. Quicken scrolls through the list to the topic you entered — or, if the topic isn't in the Index, it scrolls down to topics that begin with the same letters. If you see the topic you want information about, select the <u>D</u>isplay command button. You either see a new help screen about the topic you chose, or you see a smaller list of subtopics to choose from. If you see a subtopic list, choose a subtopic and click the <u>D</u>isplay button to get instructions on the subtopic you're interested in. Neat, huh?

By the way, if you get lost among all these Help topics, click the <u>B</u>ack button to get back where you started from.

<u>Help</u>⇨*How to* <u>U</u>*se Help*

The <u>Help</u>⇨How to <u>U</u>se Help command starts the Help application and opens a file of information about the Help application itself.

How You Use It

When you choose this command, you get a Help dialog box that is open to the Contents tab. It explains how to use the Help feature.

Help➪About Quicken

This command opens a window from which you can choose one of eight little walking tours of Quicken.

How You Use It

Get a cup of fresh coffee — maybe a cinnamon roll, too — and then choose the QuickTour you're interested in.

Help➪Quicken Tips

Choose this command to see one of those familiar Quicken Tips you get each time you start the program. Click the Next Tip button to read another tip. Click it again to read yet another tip. And so forth and so on. When you've had enough, click Done.

Help➪About Quicken

This command displays some rather esoteric information about the version of Quicken you own. It also lists some system information, most of which is hard to fathom.

The main thing to know about this command is that somewhere, someday, someone may ask you which version of Quicken you have. Likely that someone will be a tech support person. This is the place you go to find out which version you're using.

Part IV

Twenty Questions (or so)

This final part of the *Quicken 5 For Windows For Dummies Quick Reference*, 2nd Edition asks and answers a bunch of questions that people always seem to have.

1. How do I start using Quicken?

You need to install Quicken — something that isn't described
here. As part of doing this, you set up a bank account. Then all
you need to do is begin using Quicken to keep your checkbook.
You can refer to the Quicken user documentation if you want help
installing Quicken. If you want more information than the user
documentation provides, you might also want to pick up *Quicken 5
For Windows For Dummies,* 3rd Edition (IDG Books Worldwide).
I happen to know the author of that book personally, and can
assure you that he will greatly appreciate the 45-cent royalty he'll
receive when you purchase the book.

2. What should I do if I want to use Quicken in a business?

Use the Lists⇨Category & Transfer command to describe each of
the income and expense categories you want to use to keep track
of your business's financial affairs. If you want some help, get a
copy of the tax form you filled out last year or the one you'll fill
out next year. See all those lines on which you have to input
figures? You'll need to have categories set up at least for all of
these lines so that you can fill out your tax return.

Sole proprietors fill out the Schedule C form; C corporations fill
out the 1120 form; and S corporations fill out the 1120-S form.
Partnerships fill out the 1065 and K1 forms.

3. Should I do investment record-keeping?

You can if you want. Quicken has a very good investment
record-keeping feature.

If you want to do the investment record-keeping thing, you need
to set up and work with Quicken's investment account type.
(These babies can be rather complicated.) Use the
Activities⇨Create New Account command to set up the invest-
ment account. You can display investment information using the
Portfolio View window. Display this window by choosing the
Activities⇨Portfolio View command or clicking the Port icon on
the iconbar.

Let me make one final observation. If you do most of your investing in mutual funds or through tax-deferred investment vehicles such as 401(k) plans and Individual Retirement Accounts (IRAs), there's a good chance you don't need to be keeping investment records. Your mutual fund, for example, keeps track of things such as capital gains, investment income, and any expenses. And it will also calculate investment returns so that you can gauge performance. Note too that, if you're investing via tax-deferred investment vehicles, you don't have any tax-reporting requirement to track investments.

4. What if both my spouse and I want to use Quicken?

No problem. Assuming that you have separate bank accounts, you just each need to set up your accounts, one for each spouse. You can do this using the Activities⇨Create New Account command.

Let me also offer you and your spouse my best wishes for financial happiness. I think it's great you two are so open about your finances, but my guess is that you'll have one or two interesting conversations about spending. Oh yeah.

5. When should I start using Quicken?

It's great to start at the beginning of the year. Note, though, that this doesn't mean that you need to wait until next year. It's really easy to enter checks and deposits. So you might as well go back through your records and start from the beginning of the year. Okay, maybe I should say that I wouldn't do this if it's, like, close to Christmas, and you still don't have your shopping done. But if it's still pretty early in the year — say, you still haven't filed your taxes — it makes sense to go back and start at the beginning.

I should also point out that there's nothing wrong with starting at some time other than the beginning of the year. The only thing you'll lose by starting in, say, June, is that you won't have a full year of information. So it'll be harder to see how much you've really spent for the entire year. (This information can be helpful in your budgeting.) And you can't get your tax deductions from a Quicken itemized category report, nor can you export your Quicken data directly to a tax program.

6. How do I record a stop payment?

Void the check using the Edit⇨Void Transaction command. Then record a withdrawal transaction that records the stop-payment fee.

7. How do I record a check that pays more than one expense?

Good question. If you go to the grocery store and buy $50 of groceries and $5 of motor oil, you may want to split the check between your Groceries expense category and your Auto:Fuel category. You can easily do this by clicking the Splits button, which appears on both the Register and Write Checks windows. (On the Register window, it's the little button to the right of the Edit button. On the Write Checks window, it's to the right of the check, under Restore). When Quicken opens the Splits dialog box, enter the $50 of groceries on the first line of the dialog box as **Groceries** (or whatever) and enter the $5 of motor oil on the second line of the dialog box as **Auto:Fuel** (or whatever).

8. What about my credit card?

You have two choices. The most sophisticated way to track credit card spending is by setting up a credit card account and then recording credit card charges and payments in the same way you record bank-account withdrawals and deposits. (You can set up a credit card account using the Activities⇨Create New Account command.) The benefits of setting up a credit card account are that you keep track of how much you owe and where you spend the money. As a practical matter, if you carry a balance on your credit card, you need to use a credit card account.

If you don't carry a credit card balance from month to month, and you don't need to keep track of what you owe on a credit card, you may prefer to just record credit card spending whenever you pay the monthly credit card bill. You'll probably need to split the bill up into different categories. You can do this by clicking the Splits button before you record the transaction. Then, you'd categorize part of the spending as "Auto: Fuel," for example, and another part as "Recreation."

9. How do I record my paycheck?

You can record payroll checks in two ways. The easiest is to just record the net payroll check amount as a deposit, categorized as something such as "net wages." The benefit of this approach is that it's really easy. I like easy. So, if I had a job, I think I'd use this approach. (I guess I'd figure the payroll accounting department was already tracking the nitty-gritty details anyway — so why duplicate their work?)

You can also record all the nitty-gritty details of your payroll check by using the Splits dialog box. If you want to do this, you record your gross pay on one line and then all the deductions from your gross pay (as negative amounts) on the other lines. This approach is more work — especially if you need to reenter all the details of each payroll check because your pay or deductions change. The benefit of going to all this work, however, is that it makes it easier to export your Quicken data to a tax program.

If you do want to collect your wages data in Quicken so that you can export it, know that what you export will have to agree to the penny (or at least to the dollar) with what your W-2 shows. Your employer sends your W-2 to the Internal Revenue Service. The IRS assumes that the numbers on your W-2 are correct. So your tax return needs to show the W-2 numbers.

10. How do I handle cash-machine withdrawals?

You need to record cash-machine withdrawals as withdrawals from your bank account, of course. In the register's Num field, choose ATM (for "automated teller machine").

The tricky thing about cash withdrawals is how to categorize them. If you withdraw, for example, $20 and then go out and spend this money on sushi and sashimi at a Japanese restaurant, you can categorize the withdrawal as "Food" or "Eating Out" or something like this.

If you withdraw a bunch of money that you'll spend in more than one way — $200 of spending money for the month, say — you may want to be able to track the ways you spend the cash: $100 for groceries, $20 for gasoline, $32.87 on lunches and lattes, and so on. You can record these details either by splitting the cash-machine withdrawal, using the Splits button, or by setting up a special cash account using the Activities⇨Create New Account command.

11. How do I balance a bank account?

When you next get your bank statement, start Quicken, open the account you want to reconcile, and use the Activities⇨Reconcile command or click the Recon icon on the iconbar. Basically, what you need to do is verify that the difference between your records and the bank's record stems from uncleared checks and deposits (in other words, checks and deposits you know about but that the bank doesn't know about).

12. What if I can't get my bank account to balance?

This whole bank-account-balancing thing is problematic, unfortunately. If you've tried to balance your bank account before, and you've never actually been able to get the account to balance, you're not going to have much better luck with Quicken. The problem is that you don't have — or can't be sure you have — good, accurate financial records.

In this case, I have two ideas for you. First, if you're just setting up Quicken, enter the beginning bank-account balance as the ending balance from the bank statement and then enter the uncleared checks and deposits that you know aren't included. For example, if you're going to start using Quicken as of January 1, use the December 31 ending bank-statement balance and then enter all the checks and deposits that don't show up on the December statement but that you know about. By following this approach, you're almost sure to have an easier time reconciling your account. I'm Steve Nelson, and I guarantee it.

Here's my second idea. This is for people who have been using Quicken for a while but can't get an account to balance. My idea in this case is that you try to reconcile your account and get as far as you can. Then write down the unexplainable difference between your records and the bank's records. Say it's $43.52. Then repeat this reconciliation for the next couple of months.

What should happen is that in month 2 and in month 3, you'll find there's still this $43.52 difference. You'll also know that either your records or the bank's records are wrong by $43.52. Without knowing you or your bank, I'm going to venture the guess that your records are in error. What you can do is adjust your bank account balance by $43.52 so that it agrees with the bank. (If you think the bank made the error, you can also try to get it to adjust its balance.)

13. How do I export my Quicken data to a tax program?

You produce a tax schedule report by using the <u>R</u>eports⇨<u>H</u>ome⇨ Tax <u>S</u>chedule command. After you produce the report, you click the E<u>x</u>port button and fill in the dialog box that Quicken displays.

TIP

Let me make one observation. I don't think it's worth it to export Quicken data. I think it makes more sense to print an itemized category report (or some other report that tallies tax-deduction categories) and then use the information this other report shows to fill in the blanks on your tax return. You'll probably only need to pull a handful of numbers out of Quicken, anyway.

Index

• A •

Account Balances report, 146
account balances, future
    forecasting, 157–159
Account List window, 105
accounts
    creating new, 24–26, 75–77
    investment, 84–86
    liability, 91
    listing, 105–106
    moving between transfers, 68–69
    multiple bank, 181
    opening, 26–27
    recategorizing, 99–101
    reconciliation report, 154–155
    reconciling, 80–84
    summary report, 144
    tax-deferred, 77
accounts payable by vendor
    report, 137–138
accounts receivable by customer
    report, 138–139
Activities Menu commands, 73–104
Activities⇨Create New Account
    command, 24, 75–77
Activities⇨Financial Calendar
    command, 88–91
Activities⇨Get Online Data
    command, 80
Activities⇨Homebase command,
    74–75
Activities⇨Loans command, 91–97
Activities⇨Order Checks
    command, 103–104

Activities⇨Portfolio View
    command, 97–98
Activities⇨Recategorize command,
    99–101
Activities⇨Reconcile command,
    10, 80–84
Activities⇨Reconcile Card Bill
    command, 82
Activities⇨Reminders command,
    102–103
Activities⇨Update
    Balances⇨Update Cash
    Balance command, 84–86
Activities⇨Update
    Balances⇨Update Share
    Balance command, 86–88
Activities⇨Use Calculator
    command, 101–102
Activities⇨Use Register command,
    8, 78–80
Activities⇨Write Checks
    command, 8, 77–78
Add-Ons menu commands, 168
Advanced AutoCreate dialog box,
    157–158
amortization schedule, 92
annualized yield, 132
Archive File dialog box, 32
archives, year-end, 31–33
ATM (automated teller machine),
    recording withdrawals, 183
Automatic Backup dialog box, 38, 51
Automatically Create Forecast
    dialog box, 157–158

checks from Register window, 79
profit & loss statement, 135–137
program
  customizing, 69–73
  displaying version number, 177
  exiting, 51
  starting, 7

• *Q* •

QIF (Quicken Interchange Format)
  files, 41–43
QIF Export dialog box, 43
QIF Import dialog box, 42
QuickBanking service, 80
Quicken Find dialog box, 67
Quicken Interchange Format (QIF)
  files, 41–43
Quicken Password dialog box,
  35–36
Quicken
  basics, 6–7
  business uses, 180
  buttons, 13–21
  command reference, 23–177
  customizing, 69–73
  displaying version number, 177
  exiting, 51
  IntelliCharge credit card, 169
  online services, 169–173
  overview, 5–11
  preset categories, 9–10
  starting, 7
  transaction types, 8
  uses for, 6, 9–11
  using, 180
  when to start using, 181
  working with, 8–9
QuickTours, 177
QuickZoom graph
  Budget Variance, 150
  Income and Expense, 147–150
  Investments, 151–152
  memorized, 152–153
  Net Worth, 151
QuickZoom report, 121

• *R* •

Recategorize dialog box, 99–100
Reconcile Bank Statement Checking
  dialog box, 81
Reconciliation report, 154–155
records, investment, 180–181
Refinance Planner dialog box,
  163–164
Register Options dialog box, 72
Register window, 8, 78–79
  buttons, 17–18
  printing checks from, 79
registers
  editing, 55–56
  inserting blank rows, 55, 58–59
  navigating, 55
  opening, 78–79
  printing, 49–50
  reconciling bank accounts, 80–84
Reminder Options dialog box, 73
Reminders window, 102–103
Rename Quicken File dialog box, 30
Report Options dialog box, 72
Report Printer Setup dialog box,
  44–45
Report window, 121–123
  buttons, 19
Reports menu commands, 120–155
reports
  A/P by Vendor, 137–138
  A/R by Customer, 138–139
  Account Balances, 146
  Account Summary, 144
  Balance Sheet, 141
  Budget, 145–146
  Business Comparison, 142–143
  Cash Flow, 123–124, 137
  Comparison, 144–145
  exporting Tax Schedule, 185
  financial overview, 120–123
  income/expense categories by
    class, 139–140
  Investment Transactions, 134–135
  Itemized Categories, 125–126
  Job/Project, 139–140

(continued)

Notes

Notes

DUMMIES PRESS™

IDG BOOKS

10/01/95

The Internet For Macs® For Dummies® 2nd Edition	by Charles Seiter	ISBN: 1-56884-371-2	$19.99 USA/$26.99 Canada
The Internet For Macs® For Dummies® Starter Kit	by Charles Seiter	ISBN: 1-56884-244-9	$29.99 USA/$39.99 Canada
The Internet For Macs® For Dummies® Starter Kit Bestseller Edition	by Charles Seiter	ISBN: 1-56884-245-7	$39.99 USA/$54.99 Canada
The Internet For Windows® For Dummies® Starter Kit	by John R. Levine & Margaret Levine Young	ISBN: 1-56884-237-6	$34.99 USA/$44.99 Canada
The Internet For Windows® For Dummies® Starter Kit, Bestseller Edition	by John R. Levine & Margaret Levine Young	ISBN: 1-56884-246-5	$39.99 USA/$54.99 Canada

MACINTOSH

Mac® Programming For Dummies®	by Dan Parks Sydow	ISBN: 1-56884-173-6	$19.95 USA/$26.95 Canada
Macintosh® System 7.5 For Dummies®	by Bob LeVitus	ISBN: 1-56884-197-3	$19.95 USA/$26.95 Canada
MORE Macs® For Dummies®	by David Pogue	ISBN: 1-56884-087-X	$19.95 USA/$26.95 Canada
PageMaker 5 For Macs® For Dummies®	by Galen Gruman & Deke McClelland	ISBN: 1-56884-178-7	$19.95 USA/$26.95 Canada
QuarkXPress 3.3 For Dummies®	by Galen Gruman & Barbara Assadi	ISBN: 1-56884-217-1	$19.95 USA/$26.99 Canada
Upgrading and Fixing Macs® For Dummies®	by Kearney Rietmann & Frank Higgins	ISBN: 1-56884-189-2	$19.95 USA/$26.95 Canada

MULTIMEDIA

Multimedia & CD-ROMs For Dummies® 2nd Edition	by Andy Rathbone	ISBN: 1-56884-907-9	$19.99 USA/$26.99 Canada
Multimedia & CD-ROMs For Dummies® Interactive Multimedia Value Pack, 2nd Edition	by Andy Rathbone	ISBN: 1-56884-909-5	$29.99 USA/$39.99 Canada

OPERATING SYSTEMS:

DOS

MORE DOS For Dummies®	by Dan Gookin	ISBN: 1-56884-046-2	$19.95 USA/$26.95 Canada
OS/2® Warp For Dummies® 2nd Edition	by Andy Rathbone	ISBN: 1-56884-205-8	$19.99 USA/$26.99 Canada

UNIX

MORE UNIX® For Dummies®	by John R. Levine & Margaret Levine Young	ISBN: 1-56884-361-5	$19.99 USA/$26.99 Canada
UNIX® For Dummies®	by John R. Levine & Margaret Levine Young	ISBN: 1-878058-58-4	$19.95 USA/$26.95 Canada

WINDOWS

MORE Windows® For Dummies® 2nd Edition	by Andy Rathbone	ISBN: 1-56884-048-9	$19.95 USA/$26.95 Canada
Windows® 95 For Dummies®	by Andy Rathbone	ISBN: 1-56884-240-6	$19.99 USA/$26.99 Canada

PCS/HARDWARE

Illustrated Computer Dictionary For Dummies® 2nd Edition	by Dan Gookin & Wallace Wang	ISBN: 1-56884-218-X	$12.95 USA/$16.95 Canada
Upgrading and Fixing PCs For Dummies® 2nd Edition	by Andy Rathbone	ISBN: 1-56884-903-6	$19.99 USA/$26.99 Canada

PRESENTATION/AUTOCAD

AutoCAD For Dummies®	by Bud Smith	ISBN: 1-56884-191-4	$19.95 USA/$26.95 Canada
PowerPoint 4 For Windows® For Dummies®	by Doug Lowe	ISBN: 1-56884-161-2	$16.99 USA/$22.99 Canada

PROGRAMMING

Borland C++ For Dummies®	by Michael Hyman	ISBN: 1-56884-162-0	$19.95 USA/$26.95 Canada
C For Dummies® Volume 1	by Dan Gookin	ISBN: 1-878058-78-9	$19.95 USA/$26.95 Canada
C++ For Dummies®	by Stephen R. Davis	ISBN: 1-56884-163-9	$19.95 USA/$26.95 Canada
Delphi Programming For Dummies®	by Neil Rubenking	ISBN: 1-56884-200-7	$19.99 USA/$26.99 Canada
Mac® Programming For Dummies®	by Dan Parks Sydow	ISBN: 1-56884-173-6	$19.95 USA/$26.95 Canada
PowerBuilder 4 Programming For Dummies®	by Ted Coombs & Jason Coombs	ISBN: 1-56884-325-9	$19.99 USA/$26.99 Canada
QBasic Programming For Dummies®	by Douglas Hergert	ISBN: 1-56884-093-4	$19.95 USA/$26.95 Canada
Visual Basic 3 For Dummies®	by Wallace Wang	ISBN: 1-56884-076-4	$19.95 USA/$26.95 Canada
Visual Basic "X" For Dummies®	by Wallace Wang	ISBN: 1-56884-230-9	$19.99 USA/$26.99 Canada
Visual C++ 2 For Dummies®	by Michael Hyman & Bob Arnson	ISBN: 1-56884-328-3	$19.99 USA/$26.99 Canada
Windows® 95 Programming For Dummies®	by S. Randy Davis	ISBN: 1-56884-327-5	$19.99 USA/$26.99 Canada

SPREADSHEET

1-2-3 For Dummies®	by Greg Harvey	ISBN: 1-878058-60-6	$16.95 USA/$22.95 Canada
1-2-3 For Windows® 5 For Dummies® 2nd Edition	by John Walkenbach	ISBN: 1-56884-216-3	$16.95 USA/$22.95 Canada
Excel 5 For Macs® For Dummies®	by Greg Harvey	ISBN: 1-56884-186-8	$19.95 USA/$26.95 Canada
Excel For Dummies® 2nd Edition	by Greg Harvey	ISBN: 1-56884-050-0	$16.95 USA/$22.95 Canada
MORE 1-2-3 For DOS For Dummies®	by John Weingarten	ISBN: 1-56884-224-4	$19.99 USA/$26.99 Canada
MORE Excel 5 For Windows® For Dummies®	by Greg Harvey	ISBN: 1-56884-207-4	$19.95 USA/$26.95 Canada
Quattro Pro 6 For Windows® For Dummies®	by John Walkenbach	ISBN: 1-56884-174-4	$19.95 USA/$26.95 Canada
Quattro Pro For DOS For Dummies®	by John Walkenbach	ISBN: 1-56884-023-3	$16.95 USA/$22.95 Canada

UTILITIES

Norton Utilities 8 For Dummies®	by Beth Slick	ISBN: 1-56884-166-3	$19.95 USA/$26.95 Canada

VCRS/CAMCORDERS

VCRs & Camcorders For Dummies®	by Gordon McComb & Andy Rathbone	ISBN: 1-56884-229-5	$14.99 USA/$20.99 Canada

WORD PROCESSING

Ami Pro For Dummies®	by Jim Meade	ISBN: 1-56884-049-7	$19.95 USA/$26.95 Canada
MORE Word For Windows® 6 For Dummies®	by Doug Lowe	ISBN: 1-56884-165-5	$19.95 USA/$26.95 Canada
MORE WordPerfect® 6 For Windows® For Dummies®	by Margaret Levine Young & David C. Kay	ISBN: 1-56884-206-6	$19.95 USA/$26.95 Canada
MORE WordPerfect® 6 For DOS For Dummies®	by Wallace Wang, edited by Dan Gookin	ISBN: 1-56884-047-0	$19.95 USA/$26.95 Canada
Word 6 For Macs® For Dummies®	by Dan Gookin	ISBN: 1-56884-190-6	$19.95 USA/$26.95 Canada
Word For Windows® 6 For Dummies®	by Dan Gookin	ISBN: 1-56884-075-6	$16.95 USA/$22.95 Canada
Word For Windows® For Dummies®	by Dan Gookin & Ray Werner	ISBN: 1-878058-86-X	$16.95 USA/$22.95 Canada
WordPerfect® 6 For DOS For Dummies®	by Dan Gookin	ISBN: 1-878058-77-0	$16.95 USA/$22.95 Canada
WordPerfect® 6.1 For Windows® For Dummies® 2nd Edition	by Margaret Levine Young & David Kay	ISBN: 1-56884-243-0	$16.95 USA/$22.95 Canada
WordPerfect® For Dummies®	by Dan Gookin	ISBN: 1-878058-52-5	$16.95 USA/$22.95 Canada

10/09/95

IDG BOOKS WORLDWIDE

Order Center: **(800) 762-2974** *(8 a.m.–6 p.m., EST, weekdays)*

Quantity	ISBN	Title	Price	Total

Shipping & Handling Charges

	Description	First book	Each additional book	Total
Domestic	Normal	$4.50	$1.50	$
	Two Day Air	$8.50	$2.50	$
	Overnight	$18.00	$3.00	$
International	Surface	$8.00	$8.00	$
	Airmail	$16.00	$16.00	$
	DHL Air	$17.00	$17.00	$

*For large quantities call for shipping & handling charges.
**Prices are subject to change without notice.

Ship to:

Name _____

Company _____

Address _____

City/State/Zip _____

Daytime Phone _____

Payment: □ Check to IDG Books Worldwide (US Funds Only)

□ VISA □ MasterCard □ American Express

Card # _____ Expires _____

Signature _____

Subtotal _____

CA residents add
applicable sales tax _____

IN, MA, and MD
residents add
5% sales tax _____

IL residents add
6.25% sales tax _____

RI residents add
7% sales tax _____

TX residents add
8.25% sales tax _____

Shipping _____

Total _____

Please send this order form to:
IDG Books Worldwide, Inc.
7260 Shadeland Station, Suite 100
Indianapolis, IN 46256

Allow up to 3 weeks for delivery.
Thank you!

IDG BOOKS WORLDWIDE REGISTRATION CARD

RETURN THIS REGISTRATION CARD FOR FREE CATALOG

Title of this book: Quicken 5 For Windows For Dummies QR, 2E

My overall rating of this book: ❑ Very good [1] ❑ Good [2] ❑ Satisfactory [3] ❑ Fair [4] ❑ Poor [5]

How I first heard about this book:

❑ Found in bookstore; name: [6]   ❑ Book review: [7]

❑ Advertisement: [8]   ❑ Catalog: [9]

❑ Word of mouth; heard about book from friend, co-worker, etc.: [10]   ❑ Other: [11]

What I liked most about this book:

What I would change, add, delete, etc., in future editions of this book:

Other comments:

Number of computer books I purchase in a year: ❑ 1 [12]   ❑ 2-5 [13]   ❑ 6-10 [14]   ❑ More than 10 [15]

I would characterize my computer skills as: ❑ Beginner [16] ❑ Intermediate [17] ❑ Advanced [18] ❑ Professional [19]

I use ❑ DOS [20] ❑ Windows [21] ❑ OS/2 [22] ❑ Unix [23] ❑ Macintosh [24] ❑ Other: [25] _____
(please specify)

I would be interested in new books on the following subjects:
(please check all that apply, and use the spaces provided to identify specific software)

❑ Word processing: [26]   ❑ Spreadsheets: [27]

❑ Data bases: [28]   ❑ Desktop publishing: [29]

❑ File Utilities: [30]   ❑ Money management: [31]

❑ Networking: [32]   ❑ Programming languages: [33]

❑ Other: [34]

I use a PC at (please check all that apply): ❑ home [35]   ❑ work [36]   ❑ school [37]   ❑ other: [38]

The disks I prefer to use are ❑ 5.25 [39]   ❑ 3.5 [40]   ❑ other: [41]

I have a CD ROM: ❑ yes [42]   ❑ no [43]

I plan to buy or upgrade computer hardware this year: ❑ yes [44]   ❑ no [45]

I plan to buy or upgrade computer software this year: ❑ yes [46]   ❑ no [47]

Name: Business title: [48]

Type of Business: [49]

Address (❑ home [50] ❑ work [51] /Company name:)

Street/Suite#

City [52] /State [53] /Zipcode [54] :   Country [55]

❑ **I liked this book!**
You may quote me by name in future IDG Books Worldwide promotional materials.

My daytime phone number is _____

IDG BOOKS

THE WORLD OF
COMPUTER
KNOWLEDGE

❏ YES!

Please keep me informed about IDG's World of Computer Knowledge. Send me the latest IDG Books catalog.